They Came to Slay

Published by 404 Ink Limited
www.404Ink.com
@404Ink

All rights reserved © Thom James Carter, 2022.

The right of Thom James Carter to be identified as the Author of this Work has been asserted by him in accordance with the Copyright, Designs and Patent Act 1988.

No part of this publication may be reproduced, distributed, or transmitted, in any form or by any means, electronic, mechanical, photocopying, recording, or otherwise, without first obtaining the written permission of the rights owner, except for the use of brief quotations in reviews.

Please note: Some references include URLs which may change or be unavailable after publication of this book. All references within endnotes were accessible and accurate as of June 2022 but may experience link rot from there on in.

Editing: Heather McDaid & Sydney Fowler
Typesetting: Laura Jones
Cover design: Luke Bird
Co-founders and publishers of 404 Ink: Heather McDaid & Laura Jones

Please note this work is unaffiliated with the official properties of Dungeons & Dragons and Wizards of the Coast.

Print ISBN: 978-1-912489-60-2
Ebook ISBN: 978-1-912489-61-9

EU GPSR Authorised Representative
LOGOS EUROPE, 9 rue Nicolas Poussin,
17000, LA ROCHELLE, France
E-mail: Contact@logoseurope.eu

Printed and bound in Great Britain by Clays Ltd, Elcograf S.p.A.

They Came to Slay

The Queer Culture of D&D

Thom James Carter

Inklings

Contents

Introduction:
Session 0   1

Part One: Here be dragons – and queers

Chapter 1:
A potted history of Dungeons & Dragons   9

Chapter 2:
The contemporary realms of D&D   17

Chapter 3:
Queerness at the source   29

A short rest   43

Part Two: Queer play, exploration, joy and creativity

Chapter 4:
The character sheet is more than a character sheet   49

Chapter 5:
The magical effects of roleplay   57

Chapter 6:
The Dungeon Master's world   71

Chapter 7:
Raise a tankard to the homebrewers, creators,
and community   79

Another short rest   89

Part Three: Queer D&D's past, present, and future

Chapter 8:
Problems & Hope   93

Conclusion:
As one journey ends, another begins   105

References   *109*
Acknowledgements   *116*
About the Author   *118*
About the Inklings series   *119*

**For Guarm and Popples;
the best adventuring party**

Introduction
Session 0

This is going to be a game I play forever, I thought to myself midway through my first ever Dungeons & Dragons session. *It's going to change my life.* As a queer nerd who'd been deeply invested in geekery since a very early age, I'd read many a fantasy book, watched many a fantasy film and series, and played many a fantasy game. But D&D was unlike any game I'd ever played before – my character could be exactly the character I wanted, full of magic and might; I could become and be my character (and vice versa) through the art and fun of roleplaying; I could make a difference in-game when in real life it often feels like I'm powerless and unable to influence change; I was collaboratively telling an absorbing, action-packed story with my friends, while laughing and joking along the way. I was part-improv actor, part-scriptwriter, part-adventurer, part-audience member. And it was nothing short of a revelation.

When I received the *Player's Handbook* as a Christmas gift – a large, hardback book that delves into the inner workings of this immersive, tabletop roleplaying game – and despite being in the tail end of my 20s, I laboured over it like I did the guide that came with *Pokémon Blue* as a 7-year-old, or over the *World of Warcraft* manual that came with the box in my teens. Although, by that point, I'd read through the *Basic Rules* and had played countless sessions, I was hungry for more; to devour any new information I could, and to simply engage with my newfound passion. To boot, the pages were peppered with incredible artwork that featured so many compelling and varied people, places, classes, spells, items – things that, to me, were completely and utterly *cool*.

After making short work of the *Player's Handbook*, I conjured up even more character concepts, looked at other people's art and creations online, commissioned artists to create bespoke character art for my characters, followed and religiously read forums where the seasoned players hung out, delved into the fun and frivolity of actual plays like *Critical Role*, brainstormed a multitude of campaign ideas and storylines, created and illustrated my own items that could be used by anybody in any campaign, spoke to anyone who showed the faintest bit of interest in D&D – all on top of actually playing the game. My initial suspicions that D&D would be a game I'd treasure and be positively impacted by were quickly proven true.

My story of falling hard and fast for Dungeons & Dragons is by no means unique; it feels as if it's actually the more common experience. It's not hard to understand why, either. In a world that often feels devoid of magic, Dungeons & Dragons offers everybody the opportunity to tap into something extraordinary and magical, to go on adventures in mystical worlds with mighty friends, and to feel a whole spectrum of emotions – including a bucket ton of joy. In my mind at least, Dungeons & Dragons can be an incredible (and incredibly fun!) hobby for all folks: it's imaginative, creative, freeing, engaging, social, silly and serious – it's all of these things, and absolutely anything else you want it to be too.

But what also struck me during my first few D&D sessions was the game's potential for queer people in particular. By its very nature, D&D provides you with the ability to create the worlds you want to create, and gives you the freedom to be whoever you want to be in those worlds. Similarly, the game can be a playground to trial or test aspects of queerness if you so wish. I myself have inevitably played with and revelled in different aspects of sexuality and gender with my characters – from my ursine, wild man asexual druid to my gay tiefling warlock who's haunted by the untimely death of his husband, to my pansexual non-binary tiefling wizard who utilises their tarot skills to make ends meet in an unforgiving city. After speaking with friends and hearing about others' experiences, it quickly became apparent that so many other folks played with, explored, and leant into queerness when playing D&D. It felt like such an interesting phenomenon worthy of celebration – and utterly deserving of a closer, longer-form look.

In *They Came to Slay*, I'll be taking the reins as Dungeon Master, guiding you through. And don't worry; you'll also be introduced to and hear from myriad other folks on this adventure. But do bear in mind, their (incredible) stories are just the tip of the iceberg – there's a hugely vast number of other LGBTQIA+ D&D experiences out there.

First, I'll lead you through a history of Dungeons & Dragons, through to the contemporary game we play today. We'll then consider how queerness is more prominent in and around D&D in the present day, and what's contributed to the shift in the game's longstanding image. We'll also explore how certain gameplay elements lend themselves to queer play, exploration, and joy – on top of discussing queer homebrewed and fan-made content, which has also helped to shift the game's image. In the book's penultimate chapter, we'll take a tour of some problematic elements in D&D's history – a necessary step if we are to have a rounded, nuanced look at the game – before looking to the future and the untold queer possibilities resting in the Forgotten Realms and beyond.

Journey with me, adventurer, on this exciting quest for knowledge. If you haven't already, make sure to don comfortable armour and pack enough rations – you'll certainly need them.

Part One

Here be dragons – and queers

Chapter 1
A potted history of Dungeons & Dragons

The story begins in a world spoilt by war, corruption, and greed: the world is planet Earth. The planet's humans have short, frantic lives; in a blink of an eye, it's over – gone. And what makes day-to-day life on this world even worse is its punitive economic system, forcing the vast majority of them to toil nearly every day, else they'd be rendered homeless, without necessary shelter or sustenance. But, despite the barbaric way of life imposed upon them, humans are also an inventive and creative lot, producing a slew of beautiful art, and many enjoyable pastimes and games – all of which make life more bearable. It's games in particular, though, that have helped humans to play, imagine, discover, experiment, and bond in ways that weren't normally possible in ordinary life.

In the year 1969 A.D., when the first humans stepped on the moon, another event took place: two men, Dave Arneson and Gary Gygax, met each other. Minnesota-residing Arneson, a student and part-time security guard,[1] and Gygax, a Wisconsin-based insurance underwriter,[2] crossed paths at Gen Con – a wargaming convention held in Gygax's town of Lake Geneva.[3] Their preferred pastime of simulating battles with figurines and mats on tables was and is by no means an unusual thing for humans; war is entrenched in their psyche, and, in many ways, remains a part of everyday life.

After losing his insurance underwriting job,[4] Gygax began creating sellable games while cobbling shoes, as to ensure he, his wife, and his children wouldn't become homeless or without food themselves. Most notably, in 1971 A.D., he produced a wargame with friend and game designer Jeff Perren called *Chainmail*. Back in Minnesota, Arneson played numerous wargames – including *Chainmail* – repeatedly with friends and fellow local gamers, but he had the idea of combining and also expanding various aspects of the games he played, and making his own additions, changes, and improvements along the way. He also affixed a deeper, richer level of both fantasy and immersion; explorable dungeons, magical objects,[5] a character experience system[6] – and, in the process, created something new entirely, which he called *Blackmoor*. While his players traversed the many dangers and dungeons of *Blackmoor*, Arneson also acted as the lead storyteller for the game, helping to advance the plot and action in real-time.

Arneson, excited by *Blackmoor* and its potential, drove his 4-wheeled land vehicle (a 'car') to Lake Geneva in 1972 A.D. and introduced the game to Gygax.[7] He, too, shared Arneson's excitement. They paired up to co-develop it into an even newer game that could be played and enjoyed by people all across the Earth (after paying a handful of coin, of course). It was Gygax, though – arguably the more pragmatic of the two – who turned Arneson's scrappy eighteen pages of initial hand-written notes and ideas into a fifty-page, followable guide for overseeing and playing their new game.[8] While typing the pages on a proto-computer (a 'typewriter'), Gygax playtested the game with local friends as well as two of his children, Ernie and Elise. Legend has it, it was Cindy, another of Gygax's children, who helped her father to settle on the new fantasy game's name: 'Dungeons & Dragons'.[9]

Dungeons & Dragons didn't excite the game publisher it was pitched to,[10] so in order to get the game out into market, the company Tactical Studies Rules (aka 'TSR'), was originated by Gygax and fellow human and wargamer Don Kaye in 1973 A.D.[11] With limited coin – around $2,400, according to the myths[12] – TSR released Dungeons & Dragons in 1974 A.D.[13]

The core concept of Dungeons & Dragons, both then and now, is this: the Dungeon Master gathers a party of brave adventurers and places them in a mystical world. To navigate these worlds, players create characters via character sheets, fleshing them out with unique names, backstories, and appearances, on top of choosing races – like dwarves and elves – and character classes – such as a deft rogue or a holy knight known as a 'paladin'. Unless their character dies and a new one has to be created, each player controls one character per campaign, and a 'campaign' is a series of sessions that could be as short as a dozen of games, or as lengthy as over one thousand games. What each character is capable of during a campaign is largely determined by the ability scores on their character sheets – with Strength, Dexterity, Constitution, Wisdom, Charisma, and Intelligence being the main abilities – as well as luck; rolling the dice reveals how hard a sword swings, how successful or unsuccessful they are when attempting to bend the iron bars of the cage they're trapped in, and so on. Through roleplay, the players co-operate to complete their heroic quests, forging connections and deepening their friendships meanwhile – and perhaps learning about themselves, too, as they gain experience and power. Every step of the way, the Dungeon Master helps narrate and advance the story, often making their own dice rolls to determine how monsters, creatures, and other people that inhabit the world retaliate or respond to the adventurers. Together, the players and Dungeon Master tell an immersive and truly epic story – perhaps over a span of several years. Considering humans' taste for stories, adventure, and battle, it wasn't long until the game was played by many humans – particularly, at the time, young men – who wanted more excitement than the human experience could offer them.

By the 1980s, Dungeons & Dragons was a fully-fledged worldwide cultural phenomenon, with kids and adults alike playing when their oppressive schooling or work hours allowed. TSR's financial figures reflected the game's immense popularity, earning revenues of millions upon millions of coin.[14] Come the '90s, the game took a major downturn, competing against new competitors appearing in the tabletop gaming market; the advancement and proliferation of video games – a medium that allows humans to see colourful, exhilarating worlds on television and computer screens rather than in their minds; and, by 1997, they also had a mountain of unsold books and debt.[15]

On its deathbed, TSR was purchased in 1997 by Wizards of the Coast[16] – a game publishing company that released *Magic: The Gathering* a few years prior; a collectable, fantasy-based card game that whipped up immediate interest and amassed much profit. Their earlier successes meant they had enough coin to resurrect the game and brand once more. By updating the game with new materials – as well as introducing the Open Gaming License (OGL) which allowed fans to publish their own fan-made D&D content and make coin from it themselves – it caused veterans to return and new players to try D&D, thus causing the brand to live another day.

But it was in the year 2014 A.D. that Wizards truly struck gold, thanks to the release of D&D's 5th edition, known as '5e'; a rules system that many argue is simpler and more accessible. It also attracted a swathe of first-time players who defied the entrenched stereotype of what a D&D player looked like. Technological advancements, too, aided D&D's second wind – social media platforms like Twitter further carved out a broad, digital community of players, and streaming platforms like Twitch where viewers could watch others play D&D caused newbies to realise how stimulating, joyous, and rewarding the game could be.

In the present day, Dungeons & Dragons is beloved by many of Earth's inhabitants – and is more popular than ever. According to Wizards' infographic covering 2020, Dungeons & Dragons has had more than fifty million players to date, that is growing by the year.[17] But there's a specific segment of humans who play, value, and find solace in the game, that I haven't yet mentioned in this short history of humans and D&D: LGBTQIA+ folks. Throughout this book, I'll often be using 'queer' as an inclusive umbrella term for all LGBTQIA+ folks, encompassed in Bonnie Ruberg's book *Video Games Have Always Been Queer*. In this sense, '"Queer" has meant different things at different times and to different people. This speaks to the word's changing nature and multivalent meaning. [...] Today, "queer" is used in two distinct yet interrelated senses. At its most basic, queer serves as an umbrella term for people and experiences that do not conform to mainstream norms of gender and sexuality. By this definition, queer encompasses all of the identities described by the acronym LGBT (lesbian, gay, bisexual, transgender) and many more, including genderqueer, asexual, and intersex—though not everyone in these categories self-identifies as queer.'[18]

When it comes to Dungeons & Dragons, queer nerds have always played at D&D tables – and also worked in a professional capacity on and around the game. And just like their straight, cisgender counterparts, they've created and played many a horned tiefling and ethereal elf, many a rakish ranger and wicked warlock. But since the 2010s onward, the queer dice-rolling, magic- and might-wielding contingent have taken up more and more space in the overall D&D community. When browsing the nerdier parts of social media sites, watching various actual plays on sites like Dropout.tv and Twitch, and seeing the kind of folks Wizards are inviting to things like streamed one-off D&D sessions (one-shots) and podcasts, it's apparent that LGBTQIA+ D&D players are more represented, visible and included than ever before. This is a cause for celebration – marginalised people being seen, heard, and valued is crucial, considering the human race's ongoing mistreatment of 'the other'. But how did this shift – especially considering Dungeons & Dragons' longstanding image as a game played by straight, cis men – occur?

This is most curious, and poses many, many questions. What, specifically, has contributed to greater queer representation, visibility, and inclusion in the overall D&D community? Is it the queer D&D-playing community themselves? Is it the internet? Wizards of the Coast? Or is it a mixture of all these things? And what makes Dungeons & Dragons alluring to queer folks, anyway? Can the game be a sandbox for queer play, experimentation, joy, and more? With the right group, can exploring and revelling in queerness be safer within these game worlds than in the physical realm of Earth?

There are so many interesting, vital questions to answer. But first, let's delve into the world of contemporary Dungeons & Dragons.

Chapter 2
The contemporary realms of D&D

Throughout its lifetime, Dungeons & Dragons has been transmogrified, adjusted, and altered. While it's retained its core concept of being something in which players and DMs can become magical and mighty (and so much more) in mystical lands, the way you actually play the game has progressively changed. To boot, the world IRL has changed, too – most notably, there have been huge technical advances, like the internet as we know it, that may have seemed to somebody in 1974 like something from a sci-fi film. But it's thanks to these various changes that D&D has clinched immense popularity in the contemporary world, and has once again secured its spot as a go-to game for fantasy nerds. Luckily, for us to explore what's changed in more detail, we don't need to travel all the way back to 1974 – but we do need to teleport to 2014.

In 2014, the 5th edition/5e rules system for Dungeons & Dragons was released to much anticipation. With its release, 5e became the de facto rules for playing and governing Dungeons & Dragons sessions – from deciphering how easily members of a party swim across a tumultuous river, to how successful or unsuccessful they are when facing monsters hell-bent on slaying them. The ethos behind bringing out new editions is to keep things fresh, while also simplifying previously cumbersome rules and mechanics, and replacing outdated material. For instance, in the 1978 Advanced Dungeons & Dragons' *Players Handbook*, women of any race once upon a time couldn't be as physically strong as men, simply because they were women.[1] Yes, as say Kae-ra the fighter you would've been a dab hand with all manner of weapons and able to wear any armour type but, as a woman, you still would've been naturally weaker, just because.

It's arguably 5e, though, that's made the game its most simple and accessible. Let's take bending bars as an example – a deed done perhaps to break in or out of some place for whatever purpose, be it heinous, heroic, or somewhere in between. Here, I'll be drawing from 1st edition – aka Advanced Dungeons & Dragons rules.

1st edition isn't viewed as particularly complex when compared with say 3rd and 4th editions, but referencing it here still serves as a good way to see D&D's mechanical evolution.

Here, a character's capacity to bend iron bars depended on their Strength ability score – the higher their ability score, the better percentile chance they had of bending bars. A character with a Strength ability score of 3 had a 0% chance of bending bars, while a character with 16 Strength had a 10% chance. The player of the 16 Strength character would have then rolled two percentile dice – both of which are 10-sided – to see if their character would've succeeded, with a cumulative roll between 1 and 10 meaning their attempt was a success. However, if they had rolled anything above 10, they would have failed. What also complicated matters was that, when a character of fighter class reached 18 Strength, they would've gained 'exceptional strength' – which increased their ability to complete feats such as bending bars more easily.[2] The player would've needed to roll percentile dice to determine how much stronger their character became, adding more numbers and percentages to the mix. The fluctuating, wide range of numbers and percentiles unnecessarily convoluted matters. From this perhaps hard to follow example alone, you may have an inkling of what things used to be like. Personally, if I were to play a Strength-based character in a 1e campaign, I would need to keep the rule book with me at all times and constantly refer back to it.

In 5e, however, the DM would simply ask for a Strength check after hearing that a player would like their character to bend bars. A Strength check is where a DM sets a Difficulty Class (DC) number for the task at hand, and the player just has to beat it. A DC of 5 would suggest the task is rather easy to accomplish, but a DC of 20 would mean it's significantly tougher. The player rolls a 20-sided die and adds or subtracts their character-specific modifiers. If they beat the DC – 5, in this example – they succeed; if they don't, they fail. Similarly, the previously complicated tasks of things like lock-picking, opening doors, and moving silently can now all be solved with easy ability and skill checks at the roll of one die. Ultimately, with 5e, there's no wrangling with percentiles or a vast range of numbers; it's almost entirely down to your rolls.

While there's unending debate about which edition is best or easiest – everyone has their favourite, and the edition they start with may always be the easiest to them – it's clear that 5e has lessened many of the nit-picky elements of the game, carved out space for more spontaneity for both the DM and the players, and made the process of learning and playing the game smoother than it had previously been. For Gwendolyn Marshall, a long-time D&D player, the 5e system is a particularly welcome development.

Marshall is a philosophy professor, game designer, co-owner of the incredible Arcanist Press which publishes supplementary content for 5e, and a trans woman. She got into D&D as an 8-year-old, when D&D had its first pop culture moment in the '80s – but, from 2002 onwards, as the responsibilities of work and family grew, she largely stopped playing, apart from browsing the latest books and attending a few game sessions here and there. In 2014, though, she invited her old group to play D&D again with her as the DM, this time using the new 5e system. She told me that 5e was not only an immediate hit with her as somebody with hands-on experience of D&D's previous systems, but also for the rest of her group. 'We all love it,' Marshall said, citing 5e's accessibility. 'Time is my most precious resource right now in my life. I work a lot, I have kids – I don't want to spend a 4-hour game session doing one round of combat. I want to tell a story, have fun, and engage in a narrative that's imaginative and is kind of an escape. The mechanics need to facilitate that experience,' she added. 'That's why 5e is my favourite.'[3]

At the same time as 5e's release, watching people game on platforms like Twitch and YouTube had become all the more common. Actual plays – web shows or podcasts in which people play tabletop roleplaying games (TTRPGs), such as Dungeons & Dragons – were rising in popularity as well. And there's one acclaimed actual play that has had a profound impact on me personally and for the general landscape of D&D: *Critical Role*.

'I would like to welcome you to Marquet,' said Matt Mercer, *Critical Role*'s Dungeon Master, as the group began their third campaign in 2021.[4] 'The year is 843 P.D., or Post Divergence. A landmass once marred by a vengeful god during the Calamity, the staggeringly twisted mountain ranges created in its wake divided the regions that have now developed into a varied and beautiful continent…' On he continues. With his vivid descriptions, he wasn't only setting the scene for the eight players at his table – it was also for the millions of viewers at home.

The show has humble roots; pre-streaming, the friend group – which consists of famous voice actors like Ashley Johnson, Laura Bailey, and Taliesin Jaffe (who is bisexual) – played D&D together in the comfort of their homes. But, when they were approached by multimedia company Geek & Sundry to stream their adventures online, they agreed, enabling fans of their acting work and D&D enthusiasts alike to tag along for the ride.

The troupe's first campaign – which ran from 2015-2017 and consisted of one hundred and fifteen roughly 4-hour episodes – has since had parts of its storyline turned into a cartoon show on Prime Video. At the time of writing, the cartoon, *The Legend of Vox Machina*, has garnered a 100% approval rating on Rotten Tomatoes. It's been very well-received to say the least – just as their actual play content has been.

Critical Role became a worldwide success in a relatively short space of time. But watching them now, despite the massive increase in production values – they're filming at a dedicated L.A. studio, intentionally designed to look like a medieval tavern rather than a West Coast production space – and after leaving Geek & Sundry and founding Critical Role Productions, it's still an intimate affair, emanating a feeling of watching your own friends playing D&D. And seeing as each homebrewed, entirely-created-from-scratch campaign contains engaging storytelling, intricate storylines, comedic hijinks, emotional rollercoasters, and dynamic combat sequences – a long, geeky soap opera, if you will – it's no wonder that *Critical Role* has had such an impact on contemporary D&D. In online nerd spaces, it's hard not to stumble across associated fan content. Twitter and Reddit, in particular, are strewn with fan art penned by professional artists; cosplayers take photos of themselves adorned in outfits resembling those of their favourite *CR* heroes; avid fans write enthusiastic threads about the latest shenanigans, deliberating what could happen next.

While *Critical Role* is an actual play sitting at the forefront of contemporary D&D, it's still but one (albeit important) part of a plethora of new media that engages people worldwide with adventure, drama, and a good dose of tomfoolery. When it comes to other actual plays, for example, there's *Dimension 20* – an anthology actual play produced by CollegeHumor – where talented and beloved D&D aficionados such as Brennan Lee Mulligan, Aabria Iyengar, and Erika Ishii (who is pansexual and genderfluid) feature. Yet another wildly popular actual play is *Dungeons & Daddies*, a podcast with a team of brilliant writers and creators behind it – the podcast's premise is that four regular dads are teleported into a high fantasy world in which they must rescue their sons. There's also *Not Another D&D Podcast* – a show whose title jokingly refers to just how many D&D actual plays are out there – of which actor and writer Brian Murphy serves as the main and lauded DM.

From more indie actual plays to ones with much higher budgets, I could fill the rest of the book with names – but there's unfortunately a word count to adhere to. Regardless, it's clear that 5e and actual plays go hand-in-hand, and such content has played a role in the game's modern day growth. There's also the fact that, for the millions of viewers at home, engaging with such media helps with learning how 5e D&D functions in a more tangible way – watching *Critical Role* helped me gain a deeper understanding of the different kinds of ability and skill checks, on top of using my combat rounds more effectively.

Of course, creating and consuming actual plays wouldn't be possible in the first place if it weren't for their wide availability online. But this isn't the only way in which the internet has bolstered the growth of contemporary D&D – there's another aspect that's important to discuss.

Today, a Dungeons & Dragons group needn't be all in the same location as they would have needed to be in 1982 – instead, each session can be facilitated purely through digital means. No longer does a group need to postpone a session if somebody's out of town for the weekend, and nor do players need to leaf through their *Player's Handbook*s, daydreaming of finding a group with whom they could traverse the multiverse. Text, video, and voice chat apps like Discord allow folks to talk to each other in real-time; dedicated TTRPG software like Roll20 and Foundry VTT enable players to visibly see the lands, cities, and dungeons their characters are exploring via on-screen maps and artwork, with rounded digital tokens placed upon said maps to simulate the game's player characters, non-player characters, and monsters; with tools like D&D Beyond, you can create and experiment with character sheets without having to print them off, no longer needing to erase the inevitable mistakes and outdated information as you level; to boot, DMs and players can more easily find like-minded people to journey with – and from a much larger pool, as well.

For those with geeky proclivities, an entire digital armoury for playing and interacting with Dungeons & Dragons has emerged. No matter whether you prefer playing over the kitchen table or online, it's an irrefutable fact that the internet has spawned multiple ways for people to get interested in and play Dungeons & Dragons, and inevitably get pulled deeper into the fandom and overall community.

The exciting wave of actual plays that invite adventurers in, the internet, and the 5e rules system that's emphasised ease and accessibility – they've all had a marked impact on the state of Dungeons & Dragons, subsequently ushering in newbies, reeling veteran back in, and growing D&D's player base to dizzying heights. As mentioned, queer people have always been present at D&D tables. To say that they hadn't would be to render them invisible and tell a warped history of queerness in and around D&D.

Thus far, we've touched on D&D's history and its contemporary evolution. But why has queerness become increasingly more prominent in and around D&D,

and what's led to a more queer-friendly image shift for the game? At the heart of these questions lies a tale of two strands: one of the base content and the publisher, and one of those who have taken to creating their own magical worlds and experiences and sharing them IRL. Let's start with the publisher.

Chapter 3
Queerness at the source

When playing Dungeons & Dragons, a cast of colourful characters is not only required to make a semi-fantastical world feel more alive and interactive, but to also help the Dungeon Master advance the campaign's storylines. These characters are known as non-player characters (NPCs), and they're voiced and played solely by the DM. The half-cut, world-weary barkeep at the inn who scoffs at your party's proclamation that they're adventurers – they're an NPC. The cloaked prince that rejected his royal duties and has gone in search of adventure, who propositions you to dispose of the guards trying to bring him back to his so-called home – he's an NPC, too. In a campaign, a group of players can meet hundreds if not thousands of NPCs, and they all ultimately impact the players' journeys in a campaign.

If the campaign the DM is running is from a published adventure – like Wizards of the Coast's *Curse of Strahd* or *The Wild Beyond the Witchlight* – the adventure's writers will have fleshed out aspects of NPCs for DMs, thereby reducing their preparation time and enabling them to jump straight into performing as that character whenever they need to. However – and even if the DM is following published adventures, as opposed to making up their own worlds with totally new characters – there has always been freedom with how the DM interprets and brings non-player characters to life. The thrill-seeking prince? She's now a princess.

The potential to infuse an NPC with queerness, then, has always been a possibility, despite what has or hasn't been stated in any published adventures that DMs use. But since the 2010s, Wizards' writers have intentionally placed out-and-out queer characters in their official published adventures and materials, unapologetically spotlighting a range of queer folk.

Jeremy Crawford is the current game architect of Dungeons & Dragons, the lead designer of the *Player's Handbook*, and an openly gay man. Since taking on more high-ranking roles at Wizards, Crawford has publicly expressed his – as well as the overall company's – commitment to queer representation and inclusion in D&D.[1] Crawford told Cecilia D'Anastasio, as noted in her article 'Dungeons & Dragons Promises To Make Its Adventures More Queer', '...publisher Wizards of the Coast is making *D&D* more gay, and why that's a great thing. Although the original game was created by two men who were, at one point, conservative Christians, the current team behind *D&D* is, 40 years later, making an effort to accommodate everyone's escapist fantasies, not just those of its earliest fans.'[2] Thus far, this has predominantly been done by including queer NPCs in the company's official published adventures, as well as the *Player's Handbook* – the all-encompassing guide for the first-time player, helping them to create a character, learn a class, choose abilities and spells, and ultimately play Dungeons & Dragons. But who are some of these queer characters, exactly? Why is their presence necessary and important? And how has including them in official materials helped reshape D&D's image as a game?

In the 2016 adventure *Curse of Strahd* – a Gothic-leaning adventure for players level 1 to 10, and an adaption of TSR's 1983 adventure *Ravenloft* – there are two men, one named Vladimir Horngaard and the other Godfrey Gwilym, both of whom are undead and were lovers in life. There isn't a singular way to portray queer characters, after all. They don't have to always be heroic – and, in some cases, like here, neither do they have to be alive. Without giving away too many spoilers, their undeath, history, and queerness can make for engaging and emotional moments in your campaign – and delivers a useful lesson for game designers concerning the three dimensional representation of marginalised folk: in all instances, it's meaningless if it's bland, tokenistic, or reduces people down to stereotypes.

Meanwhile, players who venture to the northern town of Triboar in the *Storm King's Thunder* adventure for players level 1 to 11 can come across Urgala Meltimer. Urgala's partner, Darribeth Meltimer, got lost in a vast subterranean network of tunnels and caverns called The Underdark. After Darribeth's disappearance, Urgala carved out a new life for herself as the proprietor of Triboar's Northshield House inn. When she's not serving customers, she serves as a fierce protector of the town, helping to fend off threats to Triboar with her combat prowess.

In *Waterdeep: Dragon Heist* – an adventure that takes characters level 1 to 5 on a romp in the large, prosperous city of Waterdeep – there's Fala Lefaliir. Fala is a druid, herbalist, potion seller, and a member of the Guild of Apothecaries and Physicians. In the book, it's stated that Lefaliir is a wood elf with long hair, and 'if referred to as "he" or "she" Fala gently requests to be addressed by name or as "they".'[3] Fala asking folks to use the gender-neutral pronouns of they/them when talking to them serves as a strong reminder to DMs and players that not all people, in semi-fantastical worlds as well as our real world of Earth, identify as a man or a woman, and the importance of using appropriate, aligning pronouns. The queer representation in *Waterdeep: Dragon Heist*, however, doesn't stop with Fala. In the same adventure (even the same page) are Embric and Avi – two married genasi men, with Embric being a weaponsmith and Avi being an armourer. Players can also come across Fel'rekt Lafeen, for instance – a drow who's an incredibly deft gunslinger and also a trans man.

If the player hadn't already considered it – or didn't know their characters could be queer in D&D – the text in the *Player's Handbook* and *Basic Rules* prompts the reader to acknowledge this fact. As is written in the *Player's Handbook* for 5e, 'You don't need to be confined to binary notions of sex and gender. The elf god Corellon Larethian is often seen as androgynous, for example, and some elves in the multiverse are made in Corellon's image. [...] Likewise, your character's sexual orientation is for you to decide.'[4] Of course, androgyny is an aesthetic, and non-binary is a gender identity, or lack thereof. But the text asks the reader to interrogate who exactly they want their character to be – and that allows freedom of expression to come to the fore when building a character via the character sheet. However your character appears, whatever their gender identity, whatever gender(s) they're attracted to (if any at all), they can be exactly who they are without restriction or limitation.

Vladimir, Godfrey, Urgala, Darribeth, Embric, Avi, Fel'rekt, and Fala aren't all the queer NPCs in official materials – nor will they be the last. But the fact they do exist – not physically, but certainly within the literature, within our minds, and within these semi-fantastical worlds – is vital. Queer D&D players can see and interact with characters similar to them – people who diverge from our modern world's status quo of straight and cis – and in turn feel seen themselves. The act of witnessing such characters written into the official literature – whether they play minor or larger parts in the campaign, and whether their weapon of choice is wit, sorcery, or physical strength – can be confirming and comforting, inspirational and aspirational. From a gameplay perspective, having queer NPCs can also help queer players feel more comfortable leaning into their queerness at the table – if there are others like them, even if they're NPCs played by the DM, they're no longer 'the only one'. Just like when a queer person is in a public space – a classroom, an office, a bar – and even if they're already self-assured in their queerness, simply having other queer people around can instil a greater sense of safety, confidence, and camaraderie. It can allow straight, cis players to experience and interact with queerness, too – something they may not do often or at all in their day-to-day lives, and which can help reduce the marginalisation and subsequent demonisation of queerness.

Wizards of the Coast showcasing queerness in official materials, bit by bit, also alters the overall image of the game, and perception of Dungeons & Dragons. When Wizards upped their commitment to queer representation and inclusion in their official materials, it provoked comments on social media and internet forums regarding the inclusion of unambiguous queerness as 'woke' and other variations of the word, while others praised it. While Wizards aren't exactly taking a defined political position by doing so, they are clearly expressing their values – that queer players and queer characters aren't just welcome, but celebrated in Dungeons & Dragons – a stance that can increase queer players' emotional and intellectual investment in the game.

Now, all of this isn't to say that having queer representation in official materials is reason enough for queer folks to outright fall in love with Dungeons & Dragons – nor does the peppering of queer characters mean that true equality has been reached. But, if you're predisposed to falling head over heels with the game, with all its inherent magical and deeply fun properties – or you happen to already *be* in love with the game – then the publisher adding queer characters into source material, an ultimately simple act with profound effects, can lead to an affinity developing and/or deepening, and – when you then get to dive into the homebrewed worlds that could have evolved from there – what a treat awaits.

While there could and should be impactful improvements in Wizards' wording and actions regarding some aspects of queerness – Corellon Larethian, for instance, we'll dive more into later – the results of the company's in-progress quest for more queer representation and inclusion in official materials are thus far two-fold: they're shedding the image of D&D as solely a cishet man's game, and they're also helping queer folks who are inclined to engage with the game to feel more included, seen, and valued, both in-game and out of it.

*

As the publisher of Dungeons & Dragons, Wizards of the Coast have a resounding, sonorous voice that reaches across various and different sects of society, through means including their vast online reach. When it comes to LGBTQIA+ representation and inclusion, their efforts extend past the materials they publish for D&D; they're also using their power (read: sizeable, influential platform and resonant voice) to positively impact and influence things back down on Earth.

It's been said that, since the early days, Wizards has been a company that's internally emphasised diversity and inclusion. When they bought Dungeons & Dragons from TSR and brought many TSR staff members over,

Wizards' founder and first CEO Peter Adkison spoke to them about the kind of company culture his organisation had. As Ben Riggs wrote in his *Nerdist* article 'The Story of D&D Part Two: How Wizards of the Coast Saved Dungeons & Dragons', 'One TSR employee that made the transition to Wizards, Jim Butler, remembered that when Adkison described the work environment […] he "talked about the importance of diversity and that everyone would be working side-by-side with goths, Satanists, gays, lesbians, [transgender people], and more. He stressed the importance of a discrimination-free workplace." Butler said this environment "allowed me to come out of the closet professionally."'[5] While I don't think the 'G' in LGBT stands for 'goths' – I can only put it down to it being the '90s, and the well-intentioned language concerning queerness not being as refined as the language we use now, decades on – it shows that queerness was nonetheless supported internally. It's therefore spurring to see that Wizards would continue to be outwardly vocal about their values, especially in the contemporary world.

A recent, illustrative example is 2021's Pride efforts. Jontelle Leyson-Smith, the director of diversity, equity, and inclusion at Wizards, wrote a rousing post introducing and outlining a Pride celebration that was 'bigger and more robust than it's ever been.'[6] In the post, she acknowledged the importance of accessibility, diversity, and inclusion being baked into their games ('As we've said before (and we will say again and again), we believe our games should be accessible to everyone, and inclusive of the variety of lived experiences in you, our fans.'[7]), as well as their IRL efforts. As part of their Pride events, they held a special one-shot with celebrity and influential LGBTQIA+ participants such as Omega Jones aka CriticalBard, an incredibly talented polymathic actor, musician, and TTRPG content creator, and Anthony Rapp, the award-winning actor who most notably starred in *Star Trek: Discovery* and the iconic musical and film *RENT*. I had the chance to speak to Rapp, and learned that he'd initially played D&D as a kid, but picked it up again during the first few months of COVID-19 and the consequent lockdowns. 'I'm really glad to see [D&D] is having this renaissance in popularity. […] At its core, [D&D] can really be life-changing in a very positive way,' said Rapp.[8]

What was also mentioned in Leyson-Smith's Pride post was the release of queer-centric merch. Other companies are often quite rightly critiqued for releasing rainbow-clad products – from alcoholic beverages to phone covers – purely to make a profit from queer folks. However, in this case, proceeds from sales were redirected to a good cause the company had advocated for and helped previously – Lambert House, the LGBTQ+ youth centre in Seattle. 'The Lambert House is a charity that is near and dear to us at Wizards, founded in 1981 [...] to address the mental and physical health disparities faced by LGBTQ+ adolescents,'[9] Wizards wrote. 'Since then, Lambert House LGBTQ+ Youth Center has cared for, championed, and celebrated over 14,000 individual youth in the Greater Seattle Region through over 500,000 in-person service contacts.'[10]

'Pride is not a single moment, day, or month,'[11] notes Leyson-Smith in her post. '[I]t's a daily lived experience.'[12] This is undoubtedly true. LGBTQIA+ people and queerness also shouldn't be spotlighted only during Pride, but continuously, and Wizards *do* spotlight LGBTQIA+ folk year-round. Celebrity or influential LGBTQIA+ D&D lovers like Ian Alexander, who in addition to starring in *The OA* and voicing Lev in *The Last of Us Part II*, made history by playing the first canonical trans character in *Star Trek*; Saige Ryan, a host, producer, writer, Twitch partner, and TTRPG player; and Sara Thompson, a TTRPG writer and designer and creator of the Combat Wheelchair – a homebrewed wheelchair that can be used by D&D adventurers in-game, take part in streamed games and conversations, no matter the calendar date. Perhaps the most important and exciting episode of *Dragon Talk* – Wizards' D&D podcast – was with the folks from *Transplanar* – an all-transgender, POC-led, fully-homebrewed D&D campaign and actual play streamed on

Twitch, in which, among many vital topics, they discussed how they went about creating their non-colonial, anti-orientalist world. It's clear, then, that Wizards – with their vast platform – aren't shy about showcasing, highlighting, and celebrating LGBTQIA+ folks and queerness both in-game and IRL.

While the whole book could talk about Wizards, they aren't the only player in the Dungeons & Dragons scene with a large following. Routinely-used tools like D&D Beyond – an official digital toolset and game companion for Dungeons & Dragons – have considerable platforms and audiences as well, and they use it. It's worth noting that during the writing of this book, Wizards bought D&D Beyond – but the work they did beforehand highlighting LGBTQIA+ people is still worthy of exploration. Their 2021 Pride Roundtable 'Finding Your Place in D&D' is a standout example of a company bringing LGBTQIA+ people's voices to the fore, and providing them with space and audiences to share their experiences with – experiences that may either resonate or be entirely eye-opening to viewers.

Host and content producer Amy Dallen was joined by Bee Zelda, Brian Gray, Sam de Leve, and Anthony Rapp – LGBTQIA+ performers, streamers, and D&D lovers. They gave anecdotes of D&D being a positive force for people in the queer community, provided advice on how

DMs can ensure there's a supportive, inclusive atmosphere during D&D games, and discussed their hopes for the future of D&D.

While the entire conversation is brimming with sage insights, I want to quote de Leve's illuminating and incisive parting words. de Leve expertly and endearingly explains how queer people can connect, play, explore, and grow from playing D&D, while exemplifying the importance of those with larger audiences providing platforms from which marginalised voices can speak. These words can help synthesise people's thoughts – or better yet, cause people to view D&D from bold, new perspectives.

'One of the lovely things about [Dungeons & Dragons] is, not only does it facilitate social queer connections in ways that we often didn't have as a culture – like, this is a method of gathering for the introverts now, and that's very special and that's very important! – but it is also a democratised storytelling platform that allows for a wealth of queer representation that even as mainstream TV [and] film improves, has not yet reached the level of that gayness we're getting to in D&D.[13]

'There is such a surplus of these characters and these stories and just, gender, gender everywhere [...] and sometimes 404 gender not found. [...] Even if you don't want to play at a table yourself [and just watch actual plays instead], the queer stories that are happening in this space are ones that you can't find anywhere else, and maybe that thing that your heart was longing for – that a script has never quite captured – is going to be out there, and it may well be in D&D.'[14]

There's already so much to behold and celebrate in regard to queerness and Dungeons & Dragons – and looking at what the game's modern-day publisher is doing is just the beginning. We've still got more journeys to tread; those that leave the pages of official materials and occur within the realms of our own creativity, or are crafted by countless talented creators and homebrewers. Onwards.

A short rest

Adventurer, we've already travelled a great distance – so let us quickly rest before embarking on the next part of the journey. Warm yourself by the campfire as I explain what's coming…

If you've rolled high on Perception, you'll have noticed that throughout our short quest thus far, I've been referring to the worlds of Dungeons & Dragons as 'semi-fantastical' rather than fantastical outright. This is with good reason: the worlds that are occupied in D&D, and many other tabletop roleplaying games, too, are never purely fictitious; humans carry over so much of themselves and their realities – from how the world they're exploring visually appears, to how its political and economic systems work, to the beings and monsters that inhabit them. They imbue it all with aspects of what they know, what they see and often would like to see more of, and what they experience or would like to experience during their lives on Earth. Simply put, when Dungeons & Dragons is played, 'reality' and 'fiction' blur, each session transporting the players to a new plane that is a mix of the two.

Dungeons & Dragons, however, is still a game at its deepest core. So that it can be functional and playable for folks all across Earth, various rules, mechanics, and elements for gameplay are necessary. But what's especially interesting, adventurer, is not only how some of these gameplay elements make for a more exciting, immersive, and engaging game, but how, for queer folks, they can also be real world tools. Creating a character via the character sheet or roleplaying in first- and third-person can help curious players to explore queerness in a safe way that affords them both closeness and distance. Such elements can also be used to play with and lean into queerness in ways that may not be possible – or, at least, can be harder to do – in real life. While numerous D&D gameplay elements can be beneficial for queer players – I have a suspicion that even combat can be useful! – it's the character sheet and the act of roleplay that we'll largely be focusing our efforts on during this leg of our short quest.

But before we do proceed, it's important to state that the queerness can only be properly engaged with when the group at the D&D table isn't composed of folks who are, in brief, bigots: a safe, supportive space IRL is necessary, which we'll, of course, discuss in greater detail.

Afterwards, we'll raise a tankard to the queer homebrewers, content creators, and community, who themselves have contributed even more significantly to D&D's image shift by creating the worlds and stories they want to see by combining creativity, queerness, and D&D in exciting, engaging, and joyful ways.

Now, adventurer, let's continue onwards before time escapes us.

Part Two

Queer play, exploration, joy and creativity

Chapter 4
The character sheet is more than a character sheet

When we think about the act of playing Dungeons & Dragons in person, the image that's often conjured is a group of friends around a table with character sheets, dice, miniatures, a battle mat/board, and the Dungeon Master's screen. These are all necessary items required to play D&D IRL, and are recognisable parts of the iconography. Despite the character sheet merely appearing as just that – written- and drawn-on sheets of paper, perhaps lovingly wrinkled and accidentally torn over time (unless you're using an iPad or a laptop, of course) – it, in fact, yields remarkable properties for queer folk: the character sheet can be an outlet to unleash imagination, and the starting point for where various aspects of queerness can be explored and leant into by players, secretly or otherwise, in a world away from planet Earth.

If you haven't yet had the pleasure of filling a D&D character sheet and the creative euphoria of bringing a character into semi-real existence, the character sheet usually isn't just a page, but rather three. The first page includes boxes for you to write down your points for abilities like Strength and Intelligence, your Armour Class, and your hit points, while also providing space for noting the other important things – like your language proficiencies and carriable equipment – that help your character navigate and function in a world where scoundrels, combat, and treacherous terrain are aplenty. On top of these nuts and bolts which can later impact how you roleplay your character, the first page also prompts the player to consider and confirm their character's personality traits, ideals, bonds, and flaws – integral social, mental, and spiritual aspects of a fleshed-out being who you'll later roleplay.

It's the second page of the character sheet, though, where players are specifically asked to visualise the character they'd like to inhabit and become while playing D&D, and are provided with boxes to describe or draw their unique vision. What colour are the character's eyes? What height do they stand at? What's their weight? What about their hair – and what style is it in (if they have hair at all, that is)? What is the character's general appearance; what kind of armour or clothing do they wear? There are infinite possibilities for what you can fill these blank boxes with, even when following the art in the official *Player's Handbook* for how a certain race can look, rather than opting for your own take on a race or even going with a homebrewed race, like sharkfolk[1] or mousefolk.[2] The second page's blank spaces, which also provides room to write your character's backstory and other features and traits, enable people to brazenly experiment with queerness without confine – and, in the process, can potentially help us recognise who we'd prefer to be in real life. The character sheet, then, can be an effective, low-risk, and ultimately safer starting point for folks to test the waters of queerness before any – *if* any! – commitments are made IRL.

Gwendolyn Marshall – who discussed her penchant for the 5e system earlier – is somebody for whom character creation was a jumping point for gender exploration. 'I've absolutely explored my gender identity in roleplaying games before coming out as a trans woman myself,' she said. 'I'd say about ten or fifteen years ago, I just started choosing women avatars in video games. And when I started playing D&D again, my first character was a masc boy elf. But on a second campaign that went on for 3 or 4 years, my character was a femme character –

a deep gnome wizard – and she's still my favourite character. I loved that energy, of being and playing that role.'[3]

Marshall divulged that what was compelling about the character was her mixture of intelligence and irreverence – and that creating and then playing the deep gnome wizard helped Marshall to understand that, not only was she attracted to femmes with a similar attitude IRL, but it was something she wanted to lean into herself. 'I've always been attracted to a certain kind of femme archetype in literature and film – the smart but irreverent, badass, punk rock girl. At the time, when I was living as a man, I just thought that was my type. But I've since learned that there's a saying in some lesbian communities where they say, "I can't tell if I want to be with her or if I want to *be* her," and now I know it's actually both. But I didn't realise that until I continually inhabited those characters,' she said. What's also interesting about Marshall's time playing her deep gnome wizard was that her campaign was more geared toward dungeon crawling than queer exploration, but Marshall's experiences happened regardless. 'I noticed as well that roleplay had nothing to do with gender or sexual orientation; we were killing monsters in dungeons – we weren't playing a roleplaying game that was focused on romantic or sexual encounters or interaction. It was just a way of being that I was playing with – and I loved it.'

Lynne M. Meyer is an award-winning TTRPG creator, and a bisexual, autistic, genderfluid, chronically ill, and polyam femme who uses she/her and they/them pronouns – she, too, has played Dungeons & Dragons and other TTRPGs in exploratory ways with her characters. 'All of my characters have explored queerness in some fashion,' they said. 'As it happened, right around the time that [my husband] North invited me to my first campaign, I was in the process of coming out to myself as bisexual. North and I are polyamorists, and have been since the early months of our dating. It was new to me, but familiar territory for him, and somewhere in our relationship journey, I had the life-changing realisation that I wasn't actually straight.

'North has always not only been incredibly supportive of my queer identity, he's also one of the most truly inclusive individuals I've ever known — and that's reflected in the games he runs. His GM style and the game worlds he creates have made it easy for me to get to know myself better, especially in those first few years. I made the deliberate choice to make my first character bisexual; playing her gave me the opportunity to begin to figure myself out as a queer femme long before I had a real-life same-gender relationship. With really just two exceptions, all of my characters have also been bi femmes.' In addition to exploring and leaning into bisexuality, Meyer and her characters in D&D and other

TTRPGs have grappled with gender. 'With my mostly straight character Orianna, I primarily chose to explore gender roles and expression, as she was a tall, strong, human fighter who kept running into challenging situations because of what others assumed that her physicality and her gender expression meant about her. She spent a good deal of time figuring herself out, exploring her identity, attractions, and desires as she wrestled with others' perceptions of her. This was also part of my personal journey, although I wasn't entirely conscious of it at the time and didn't have — and still don't quite have — the language for that part of my identity. I've since come to realise that although AFAB [assigned female at birth], I really don't identify that way much of the time. Today, I consider myself genderfluid, and use both she/her and they/them pronouns depending on the day and situation.'[4]

Fiona Reid, a public sociology student at Queen Margaret University, researcher, and avid D&D player, started with another TTRPG – *World of Darkness*, the same Meyer started with too – before playing and falling in love with Dungeons & Dragons. On playing D&D for the first time and making her first-ever character, she said, 'There was something so magical about being whoever you wanted to be. I went for the very typical horny tiefling bard for my first character, and it was so fun to explore that side of myself.'[5] As somebody who's in a long-term monogamous relationship with a man, D&D has proven to Reid to be an effective avenue for exploring her bisexuality. 'D&D has been one way I have been able to explore my own bisexual identity in a safe and fun way. I've been able to create lesbian or bisexual characters who have relationships with women – all sorts of relationships! Hookups, long-term, anything in between. It's been great to explore that through the game, while also getting to be an absolute badass and feel unstoppable while doing it. I think especially because I didn't realise my own queerness properly until I was already in a relationship with a man, this was really important for me developing my own queer identity.' Reid now DMs a homebrewed D&D campaign for a group of eight players, and seeing them create and play their own queer characters without hesitation is something that's been gratifying for her. 'I love seeing my players explore their own identities and get to play out aspects of themselves they may not be able to in real life. Many of my players have non-binary characters, or characters that are otherwise LGBT, and it's so fun to get to watch them exist in a world where that's just fine and there's never any prejudice or worry that someone might not accept them for their identity.'

Ultimately, the character sheet – whether physical or digital – is more than a character sheet; a character is more than a character; fantasy is never just fantasy, but so much more. Regardless of who we are in the real world, we bring so much of our lives to our D&D sessions – and not least when it comes to our characters. Out in the real world, experimenting with or sometimes simply leaning into queerness can be outright dangerous or unpredictable in many places and spaces. But Dungeons & Dragons' three-paged character sheet can be the springboard to gently interrogate and revel in queerness with reduced risk and without ongoing commitment. Whether you create and play a tiefling ranger who's non-binary because you have a suspicion that you don't subscribe to the concept of the gender binary either, or a devastatingly handsome dragonborn bard who's pansexual because you're questioning your own sexual orientation and where you sit on the spectrum, the character sheet helps queer folks to not only create three-dimensional characters in D&D, but it can also even help you become the most realised, you-est you out of the game, too. You can become the (game)master of your own destiny. And that's magical.

Chapter 5
The magical effects of roleplay

After being told that The Lower Order's leader, Braithe, was ready to meet with Okin, Okin briefly left the rest of his party – Pem, Lux, Cleaver, and Brother Keith – at their impromptu camp by a grassless hill. Walking towards the hill, and through an unnatural black haze, he could just about see some kind of statue – a towering, inanimate skeletal figure, made out of fresh-looking humanoid-sized bones. Where its heart should be, the statue somehow emitted the coarse, cough-inducing haze, which completely obscured the nearby surroundings. Nobody could really tell what time of day it was – it could've been daybreak; it could've been midnight.

The Lower Order's sickly-looking lackeys directed Okin to a decaying, church-like building mere steps away. Opening the church's entrance door, and despite there being no light source, he swore he saw a dozen sullen, humanoid eyes staring back at him. But who they were and how far away they were, he couldn't say. He used his hands to guide him around the building, occasionally hearing the sound of shuffling across the stone floor. Eventually he found the stairs, walked down them, and reached a door that opened up to a dimly-lit underground study – and saw Braithe for the first time in over a decade.

'I must say, I'm surprised to see you again after all these years,' said Braithe while standing next to his desk – a surfeit of tomes and skulls scattered upon it. As he spoke, Braithe smiled a hollow smile; instantly, Okin knew there was something wrong – years ago, back home in the city of Vessila, Okin began to witness him following a nefarious path. Judging by the menacing, towering figure outside and his change in demeanour, it was apparent that Braithe's harnessing of and obsession with necromantic magick had indeed taken him down such a path – one which could spell disaster for Eythur.

'You've hardly changed since I last saw you, Braithe,' said Okin, further taking in the sight of the study as he spoke. 'We both still look so similar, but perhaps with more grey in our hair...' But before Okin could continue, screaming could be heard from outside, and the deathly smell of necromantic magick seeped in. The two men looked at each other; Okin with confusion in his eyes, Braithe with knowing.

'Okin, you wrote a harsh letter to the entire Vessila Magick Council, stating your disapproval of my interest in necromancy. Because of that letter, I was banished from Vessila, and the few who saw the true potential in necromancy magick followed me. While you and your little troupe have been running around Eythur, taking out other groups you believe to be working with the liches of the underworld, I've been watching – and waiting. I know you well, remember? We were the closest of friends for many years. You wouldn't think I'd simply let you and your new friends waltz in and try to halt what we're doing, too?' As Okin began to realise the trap that his old friend – who was a brother, really – had laid, he heard the unmistakable, guttural screams of his mighty friend, Cleaver, from outside. His friends were either thwarting the ambush from The Lower Order and their necromantic magick – or succumbing to it.

*

This scene is a memorable moment from an ongoing, privately homebrewed campaign of mine that began in 2021 – my group's Dungeon Master and I were roleplaying as Braithe and Okin respectively. Roleplaying – the act of performing as a character; thinking as they would, improvising their speech in response to player characters and non-player characters alike, and stating their in-game actions and explaining how they navigate through the world – is what brings the game of Dungeons & Dragons alive, imbuing it with soul where mechanics, such as rolling dice and adding up numbers, simply doesn't. As Daniel Mackay wrote in his 2001 book *The Fantasy Role-Playing Game: A New Performing Art*, 'Rules and game mechanics may make the arbitration of a session either satisfyingly graceful or frustratingly confusing, but it is the performance of the session that brings the game to life.'[1]

Roleplaying can be boiled down to acting. But when roleplaying in a game like Dungeons & Dragons, the roleplayer needn't have any theatrical training or acting experience. Instead, all that's required is engagement as well as the shedding of self-consciousness; to fully lean into the voices, gestures, and the world the journey takes place in. After all, no other Earthly activity is nerdier than this – you might as well have fun with it.

When roleplaying in Dungeons & Dragons, there are predominantly two ways of going about it: first-person roleplay, where you speak directly as your character ('You've hardly changed since I last saw you, Braithe...' or 'I walk down the staircase to in an attempt try and find Braithe...') and third-person roleplay, where you narrate what your character does ('Okin walks down the staircase in an attempt to try and find Braithe...'). Unless you strictly use only one form, you'll usually swap, without noticing, between both first- and third-person roleplay, deepening your character's individuality, selfhood, and presence – session after session – as you do.

As you play, there will be arcs in the campaign that will require an emotional response from the character you're roleplaying: perhaps they've reunited with a long-lost friend or family member, or maybe they've witnessed a fellow adventurer perish by the skeletal hands of a vengeful lich. To accurately and convincingly portray the emotions a character is feeling in any given moment – and as if for the very first time – theatre, television, and movie actors and performers tap into the lived experiences that they've had. Richard Schechner, a performance theorist, director, and University Professor Emeritus at the Tisch School of the Arts, New York University – and whom Mackay references in his book – refers to these stored-up emotions as 'restored behavior'[2] or 'strips of behavior'[3] – behaviour that can be recalled at a whim during a performance. Roleplayers can do this too, tapping into their wellspring of previous experiences, thoughts, feelings, and reactions if they need to. They can also simply live in the moment, reacting exactly as their characters would feel in that very instance, whether the predominant emotion would be shock, joy, sadness, excitement, or something else entirely.

As an experienced, award-winning actor himself, the aforementioned Anthony Rapp is no stranger to performing and playing – but he was drawn to roleplay in an unexpected way. 'One of the things I've really fallen in love with in D&D as an adult is the roleplaying aspect – which I didn't anticipate needing or wanting as much because I get to do that in my work. But it's a different use of those muscles – and it's been really rewarding in ways that I would never have predicted,' he said. One especially memorable moment, he told me, happened while playing in a campaign with fellow *Star Trek: Discovery* cast members, during some downtime from filming. 'It was this very intense session where we had this huge battle and one of us almost died – and we had this whole unpacking about it. My character and Mary Wiseman's character had a really profound disagreement about what went down and how it went down, and we were both fully in that moment. There were ways that my character was behaving in that moment that I don't know that I would in life, and I think the same thing for Mary. But we were exercising these new ways of expressing ourselves within a safety net. And that was an astonishing thing,' Rapp said. 'In a rehearsal process, there are times where you can improv a little bit, but it's always within those confines – you're still working within the framework of the play or musical's overall plot. But in the storytelling in D&D, anything can happen any time. Being with a group that you really trust and have a sense of safety with, you're safe to stretch yourself, your ways of thinking, take risks, and even practice muscles that could aid you in life.'[4]

Roleplaying, then, is a heady mixture of emotion and immersion – it's also an activity where you become a character who's, say, the polar opposite of you, or even perhaps a more idealised version of you: the possibilities vary wildly, and it all depends on the kind of character you created with your character sheet before the campaign kicked off. And while roleplaying is undoubtedly helpful for cishet players to play and explore (and gain more empathy and understanding by sensitively playing characters who are different to them), roleplay for queer folks can be especially beneficial. After all, in the real world, roleplay is a useful tool used in many spheres of life – including therapy. Just because the roleplaying here takes place within the nerdy context of Dungeons & Dragons rather than a therapist's office, that doesn't mean it can't be valuable.

If the character sheet is where you create your character and settle on their name, pronouns, gender, appearance, clothing, sexuality, class, race, background, and attitude, it's roleplay where you become the character – or they become you. For queer people who are playing Dungeons & Dragons in an exploratory manner when it comes to identity, roleplay can offer players the opportunity to voice either their or their characters' thoughts, emotions, wants, and wishes, ultimately giving the player a chance to trial and test how the textures of those things feel upon vocalising or perhaps doing them, and how deeply it all – *if* at all! – resonates internally. While a singular D&D one-shot lasting 4 hours or so may or may not provide the player with enough time, space, or opportunities to navigate questions such as 'is this merely a step into another's shoes, or do I deeply relate to and share a kinship with this character IRL?,' an ongoing campaign that takes place over months – if not years – certainly can.

There's also a conceit when it comes to roleplaying in Dungeons & Dragons, as well as other tabletop roleplaying games – the character you're roleplaying as (or them you) offers a veil to hide behind IRL, consequently masking your roleplaying simply as roleplaying rather than out-and-out experimentation. This, if the player wants, allows them to keep their cards close to their chest, helping them to go about their experimentation away from the gaze of others. It can also make for an all-round less pressured experience, too – and this is something that Posey Mehta, an actor and one of the main players of an actual play called *Trisha's Hideous Queers*, touched on: 'I think for folks who haven't yet come out to themselves, character-based play like this helps to create a sense of perceived distance: you can explore these feelings without having to confront the idea they exist within you. If it all gets too much, you can just fold up your character sheet and put it away.'[5]

When roleplaying, there's another positive process that can take place: catharsis – the purging of the feelings that we've buried deep within ourselves, and have carried around with us for perhaps an extensive amount of time, unable to fully shake off.

Unbeknownst to my DM, I intentionally based the story – the friendship, the closeness, and the eventual parting of ways – of Braithe and Okin on my own experiences. During my formative years, my best friend was a cishet guy – something rare for me both then and now, as the bulk of my friends has always been cis women and other queer folks. He later drifted away, choosing to spend less and less time with me and our shared, arty friend group for the sports-obsessed lads whose pastimes and ways of perceiving the world were radically different. Ever since, I've harboured a slight confusion around why he veered away from our once-strong friendship, as there was always vagueness in his answers whenever I asked why we weren't hanging out nearly as much. I eventually concluded, whether rightly or wrongly, that the issue was my queerness: that he, on some level, knew about my difference and it made him uncomfortable. Perhaps it was the idea that by associating himself with me, he would appear less masculine or it would somehow lessen his 'straightness'. Either way, I don't know.

When in talks with my DM about establishing a narrative backstory for Braithe and Okin, I instinctively returned to this experience and the feelings that came with it. I thought that, when roleplaying, I could unearth those emotions – the aforementioned strips of behaviour. Little did I know, when my DM and I began to roleplay and improv around Braithe and Okin – who used to be best friends back home in Vessila – I would find the experience cathartic; the art of roleplaying and the unfolding of that arc naturally led me to an emotional and mental place where I could get over our IRL diverging of paths, the dissolution of our friendship, and feel confident in my own trajectory as a queer person.

Of course, the events, experiences, and emotions we individually feel catharsis around – both in and out of Dungeons & Dragons – can differ greatly. But the fact remains, catharsis can absolutely be stumbled upon and felt in these semi-fictional worlds and with these semi-fictional characters through roleplay. And when it comes to queerness in particular, there's a whole slew of additional aspects we can feel catharsis around, whether that's something like discovering a gender identity that you identify with, or assessing and working through past events.

*

Ultimately, becoming your character, or them becoming you, through roleplay can be an incredibly powerful tool for queer D&D players, providing a safeguarded way to dig deeper into who they are, and grapple with questions that sometimes aren't so easily answered. There's also the potential to stumble upon and find much-needed catharsis along the way, too. Considering how few spaces and opportunities there are in the real world that offers us the ability to safely play, poke, and prod while wearing a guise that simultaneously affords us both closeness and distance, it's a testament to roleplay *and* the game itself.

*

'We were once such good friends, so I'll give you a choice,' Braithe said, calmly. 'You can either join The Lower Order and aid us – or, you die. I cannot have my work, what I've dedicated the past ten years to, be stopped by you or your friends. Speaking of which, it sounds like your friends won't be with us for much longer…' Okin began to seethe. He took a breath before briefly closing his eyes to assess his limited options.

Entering Braithe's study mere minutes ago, Okin noticed a runed black gem on the desk: he and his party had been told by one of Eythur's wisest magick historians that such a gem could be used to bridge the underworld with the living world, upsetting the balance of life and death and simultaneously bringing untold horrors unto Eythur. Seeing as Okin could no longer reason with Braithe, the next best option was to put a halt to his plans – it was just lucky that, for whatever reason, the gem hadn't already been used.

Okin opened his eyes. 'I've made my decision,' he said. 'We have so much history… and seeing you again brought it all back. I want to make up for lost time – and I'm sure whatever you're doing with The Lower Order is for the greater good. I'll join.' He then extended his left hand, waiting for Braithe to shake it; almost immediately, Okin's hand was shook with vigour. 'I'm so glad you've finally come around,' Braithe said, earnestly. But as the handshake reached its apex, Okin used its momentum to push Braithe over backwards, buying a few seconds in which to procure and escape with the gem. With his right hand, Okin reached out for the gem, quickly snatching it. He then dashed out the room and scrambled toward the church's entrance. As soon as he stepped outside, he used his free hand to shake his Idol of Animal Magick, which allowed him to transform into a magick-infused critter once per day – this time, he chose an owl. He tightened his talons' grip on the gem before flying through and out of the haze. Once through, he began swooping toward an uninhabited mass of nearby land. He felt a thrill course through him; while there was sadness regarding Braithe and him being too far gone, the fact that Okin's initial suspicions were correct, and that he forged his own path devoid of Braithe which he derived happiness and purpose from felt celebratory. But he couldn't ruminate for too long; the gem needed taken care of.

Okin hovered above a leafless thicket for a second before diving down. By the base of a tree, he buried the gem so that it was hidden but could be later found by the party and disposed of properly. He then began making his way back to his true friends, hoping that they'd survived the ambush. It took less than a minute to reach them again, and, when he did, he was met with the sight of Cleaver who, with his axe, divided the last remaining Lower Order lackey into two.

Chapter 6
The Dungeon Master's world

While there are numerous gameplay elements in D&D available to players with which they can investigate or simply enjoy queerness, there are also other overlapping and separate elements laden with queer potential available to the mighty conductor of all D&D games: the Dungeon Master. Creating a world, establishing and roleplaying the various people inside that world, and thinking of the subsequent campaigns and storylines are tools in and of themselves – and offer Dungeon Masters rich, varied ways of exploring, enjoying, and generally engaging with queerness.

Creating a world – whether for a one-shot or a years-long campaign – is essentially an in-depth creative writing exercise. What is the world like, geographically? How is it governed by its people and/or its gods? What do those people and/or gods do on a daily basis? Do they have any societal taboos? On the flip side, what and/or who do the world's societies exalt? These are just a few of the many, many questions that are considered and grappled with during the early stages.

For queer-minded DMs who ask themselves similar questions while homebrewing their own worlds – or adapting and altering published materials to their whim – there's the ready potential to imbue these worlds with queerness from the get-go, and from angles that are a welcome departure from what's experienced in the real world. Perhaps homophobia and transphobia, for instance, simply don't exist within your societies. Maybe all queer people are viewed as powerful beings and held in higher respect than cishet folk. Or, in terms of sexuality, maybe there's no such thing as 'straight' or 'gay,' with such concepts regarded as absurd. From a campaign and storyline perspective, perhaps your world's main city has a particularly rife criminal underbelly, with a queer organised crime gang operating in a Robin Hoodesque way for some greater good and who your adventurers bump into – for better or worse.

Intentional and thoughtful DMs usually won't go about the creation process without getting input from their players, though. And by sending the group something like a safety and consent survey before a campaign kicks off or even before the world itself is created, Dungeon Masters can understand players' gameplay preferences and gauge how comfortable they are with things like violence (blood, gore), societal and cultural issues (racism, religion, homophobia, transphobia), and even relationships and, in purely adult games, sex. On top of the survey providing the DM with information on subject matters to avoid, it can also detail the things players *would* like to see – for instance, in adult games, sex between player characters and NPCs or other player characters, and how that sex is depicted: whether it's explicitly narrated from beginning to end by those involved or if things quickly fade to black. Even if such surveys aren't sent out, eagle-eyed DMs may pick up on certain player wants and wishes during sessions – and improvisationally run with them or intentionally bake them into their sessions going forward. For Gavin McMurtrie, a queer Glasgow-based Dungeon Master who's been a part of the D&D fandom for over a decade now, serving his queer players with the queer-oriented storylines they're interested in is important – and something he does regularly. 'As a DM who's open to romance in my campaigns, I've seen a few players test the waters with exploring queerness – and I'm more than happy to oblige by working queer storylines, and just more generally incredibly queer settings, into our campaigns,' he said.[1] This is something that Robbie

Taylor Hunt, the DM of the *Trisha's Hideous Queers* actual play, also does. 'In pre-game one-on-ones, I make sure to get a sense of whether my queer players are excited about exploring romantic and/or intimate potentials in their character's story, and how that might manifest in-game,' he said. 'Then, I offer possibilities for romance and sex without them being really instrumental parts of the narrative, and/or I run with it when players orchestrate moments of flirting or attraction themselves. My caveat being that, if you as a DM aren't comfortable portraying romance or sexual relationships, either at all or of certain types, then please make that clear to your players – your boundaries and enjoyment are just as important as theirs!'[2]

Ultimately, how a DM goes about designing a world, its NPCs, its campaigns and storylines, is limitless. How ever a DM does go about it, the inclusion of queerness through these many facets can not only provide extra opportunities and experiences for players to explore, enjoy, and interact with queerness, but for the DM too.

One particular way DMs can interact with queerness is through roleplay and, more specifically, 'multi-roling'. In theatre and performance circles, multi-roling is where one actor switches between different characters in a single production, using a change of voice, clothing, and body language to infer to the audience that they're somebody new. In D&D, the DM is essentially a one-person theatre troupe where they're playing hundreds of NPCs, meaning they're constantly multi-roling.

McMurtrie himself has experience exploring queerness through the characters he's portrayed when multi-roling. 'For me, even though I do consider myself to be cis, I've experimented and explored my own gender in the past, and D&D ended up being a fantastic avenue for that,' he said. 'Being the one responsible for roleplaying every NPC the party interact with, I've been able to slip into character as the most stereotypical images of male masculinity, as hyper-feminine women, as soft boys, as butch ladies, as all manner of non-binary folk – and even some characters that – like me, at the time – were a little lost. I also feel it's safer to experiment this way, as it's totally expected the DM will be trying on a wide variety of personas over a session.'[3] As McMurtrie astutely noted, DMs have even more flexibility to wear myriad metaphorical hats – and even more inconspicuously.

The Dungeon Master, then, due to their very position as chief creator and storyteller, has the inherent power to imbue queerness into worlds, NPCs, campaigns, and storylines. As an additional, simple example: Rapp, who started DMing himself in 2022, rolls a 6-sided die to determine the gender of his NPCs; a roll of 1 or 2 means the NPC in question is a man, 3 or 4 is a woman, and 5 or 6 is non-binary. 'I wanted to make people who are non-binary ubiquitous,' he said.[4] Ultimately, there's an argument that can be made that, really, it's the Dungeon Master who wields the most tools with which they can explore, enjoy, and engage with queerness.

*

In the end, both DMs and players have a multitiude of tools (delete overlapping and separate) within Dungeons & Dragons which can engage and interact with queerness. However, folks can only do these things if the environment at the table is safe and free from bigotry in its many forms.

There's a well-used phrase in the overall Dungeons & Dragons community that 'no Dungeons & Dragons is better than bad Dragons & Dragons.' Bad (read: unpleasant, offensive, tyrannical) DMs and players of course exist. For marginalised people, instances where you're paired with an individual or potentially an entire group of folks who exhibit discriminatory or oppressive behaviour can be harmful, causing people to withdraw into themselves and become confused, annoyed, or upset – among a vast range of other emotions; and that's just the short-term effects without taking into account the medium- and long-term consequences. The in-game content that's been homebrewed and delivered by the DM could potentially be harmful too, and have similar negative consequences – even if the DM initially assumed the content in question was harmless.

But how can safe spaces be established so that queer D&D lovers – which includes both players and DMs – can engage with queerness without fear? While everybody's ultimately responsible for their own behaviour, it's largely the DM's responsibility to create, cultivate, and oversee a safe environment from the beginning. If a DM is forming a group composed of folks they don't know or who their friends can't vouch for, the aforementioned safety and consent survey is also a nifty way of filtering out people who could pose a threat to a safe environment, on top of serving its original purpose – letting the DM know what kinds of content players would and wouldn't like to see in-game. As McMurtrie told me, 'If I'm playing with someone relatively new or who I don't have much experience with, I make sure to speak with them ahead of time individually to establish where boundaries might lie, and there are some excellent consent sheets floating around [on the internet] for DMs to help with this.'[5]

Communication around expectations, boundaries, and triggers is key – and communication should continue throughout the campaign's lifespan, not just before a campaign kicks off. 'As campaigns progress, I make sure to check in regularly with each of my players away from the table, just to make sure nothing's come up or happened that made them uncomfortable,' McMurtrie said. 'On a few occasions I've had to speak to players about some language they've used, as well as adapt my own language after players have spoken to me, but ensuring that two-way communication keeps up and everyone feels respected and comfortable is key to a happy table. Unfortunately, it's not always easy, and there are a couple of players I've had to exclude from groups before because they've proven unwilling to adjust their own behaviour despite it making others uncomfortable. But as the DM, that's one of your responsibilities.'

'No D&D is better than bad D&D' rings true. A negative experience can have a colossal impact on how somebody feels about the game – to the point where they could understandably forgo it outright, never to return. But, Dungeons & Dragons can be an incredible game for all folks, and especially for nerdy queers for whom the real world is stifling or simply not enough. While roleplaying games offer a whole host of gameplay elements that have queer potential, it's only when there's a safe environment back on Earth that queerness can be delved into by its players and Dungeon Masters without drawback. And then remarkable things can happen.

Chapter 7
Raise a tankard to the homebrewers, creators, and community

Throughout history, we as queer people have always created our own spaces and forms of entertainment – sometimes out of necessity, and, at other times, simply because we wanted to. When it comes to Dungeons & Dragons, this tradition continues. The queer homebrewers, content creators, and community have done a ton of work when it comes to queerness and D&D – and with a little assistance from the internet. Their efforts offers something to adventurers of all levels – from those who have dipped their toe in the water of roleplaying, or are years-deep into a campaign, to those curious but just comfortable (for now) watching from afar. When I say remarkable things can happen, this is what I'm talking about – and it's truly the heart of the game.

Let's start with the queer homebrewers. Ever since Dungeons & Dragons was released in 1974, the art of homebrewing – that is, creating your own worlds, character races, classes, spells, monsters, even fully-fledged adventures, that aren't officially approved but produced because they're *cool*, engaging, or fun – has been part and parcel of D&D life. But the introduction of the Open Gaming License in the early '00s meant that homebrewers could be more open with publishing their materials: they won't run into legal issues (as long as they abide by the rules of Wizards' Open Gaming License and Systems Reference Document) when putting their work out there and earning money from it.

Thanks to the OGL and the internet, homebrewed content has become far more easily dispensed and accessible. It's not just relegated to being shared between friends but can be quickly found on dedicated homebrew sites like Dungeon Masters Guild and DriveThruRPG, to name just two. It's led to more people offering their works to the world – and that, naturally, includes queer-centric works by queer homebrewers.

One standout and wildly fun example is Oliver Darkshire's *Queercoded* – a compilation of queer villains (or rather, as the PDF's cover clarifies, 'misunderstood heroes')[1] that can be added to your campaign. *Queercoded* also includes 'GAY AGENDAS. BENT CAMPAIGN ARCS. LAIRS. LOCATIONS. LOVERS,'[2] which also states that the material offered is 'complex and nuanced. fickle and one-dimensional. serious or comedic. we are not a monolith – we can have all those stories, and they call [sic] *all* be queer.'[3] *Queercoded* is queer representation at its finest and fullest, showing the many facets of queer people and life.

Elminster, a campaign villain/misunderstood hero who's non-binary, goes by he/she/they pronouns, and whose gender presentation varies, is perhaps the most visually compelling and narratively chaotic of all the queer villains/misunderstood heroes in *Queercoded*. For the character art, artist Gennifer Bone has depicted Elminster as one of his many drag personas, El-Mystra. As El-Mystra, Elminster has the typical wizard traits of grey hair, a lush beard, and a pointy hat – but also blocky eyeshadow, bright lipstick, long, painted nails, and a pink fur shawl. As an antagonist, Elminster wields immense power but lacks foresight and responsibility; constantly meddling, creating drama, and getting involved with events she shouldn't, leaving death and destruction in their wake. With a fully realised stat block complete with a selection of spells, plot hooks, and methods of integrating Elminster into your campaign, Darkshire has provided a queer campaign villain/misunderstood hero that's stan-worthy – does Elminster really need to die, or will reasoning with them or coming to some sort of deal suffice?

Queercoded and Darkshire aside, examples of other LGBTQIA+ creators who've intentionally put queerness as the focal point of their homebrewed works include: Jack and Alex Dixon, creators of *Adventuring with Pride* and its sequel *Queer We Go Again*, which both include fun-filled adventures as well as new items and subclasses; Remi Permann, who wrote and published *Blessed of The Traveler: Queer Gender Identity in Eberron*, a guide for adding trans characters and stories into the Eberron D&D setting; and Jun Suau, author of *Queer Bees in a Box*, the adventure created for cottagecore sapphic players.

It's not just queer homebrewers who have utilised the internet to distribute and showcase their work – it's queer content creators, too. For definition purposes, let's use 'content creator' as a catch-all term for folks producing illustrations, actual plays, blog posts, YouTube videos, and so on – not just homebrewed materials and homebrewed materials alone.

One of my favourite scrappy, DIY, weird, fun, and audaciously queer actual plays is the aforementioned *Trisha's Hideous Queers*. The name is a pun referencing an in-game spell called 'Tasha's Hideous Laughter,' which would cause the caster's target to laugh uncontrollably and become incapacitated for up to 1 minute.[4] *Trisha's Hideous Queers*, which is watchable on YouTube, follows a rag-tag troupe – namely Bug and Bramble, with a plethora of guests along the way, including Sari who's played by Drak, a Black TTRPG streamer and content creator – as they venture out of their homes and explore a desert wasteland known as the 'Tundro' while on their shenanigan-filled quest. No matter how hard you try, D&D campaigns usually give way to chaos and comedy – and *Trisha's Hideous Queers* leans into both early on. Watching the series on YouTube, it's a delight to see the group – all of whom work in the performance industry – play, collaborate, and laugh all while causing the viewers at home to laugh, too. Serendipitous, considering the spell their actual play is referencing.

I corresponded with Robbie Taylor Hunt, Posey Mehta, and Rosanna Suppa – the DM and the main players of *Trisha's Hideous Queers* – to learn more about what inspired them, why queer-centric actual plays are important, as well as getting some of their thoughts on why queer folks are drawn to D&D and homebrewing.

The group of friends had previously played D&D together, but the idea for *Trisha's Hideous Queers* evolved when COVID-19 spread, and planet Earth began to change. 'Rosanna and I were working with The Place Bedford [a theatre] to create some game-based interactive projects which would explore queerness in some capacity for their Game Play Festival,' Taylor Hunt said. 'In our brainstorming, we'd begun to conceive of a wasteland world with protected zones and peoples roaming beyond. Due to COVID, it needed to be delivered remotely, so it became *Trisha's Hideous Queers* and a D&D 5e actual play and campaign set in the Tundro wastelands with protective Corestellation domes.'[5]

Queerness has been integral to *Trisha's Hideous Queers* from the get-go, and something that's undeniably present. 'What I love about *THQ* is that so, so much of it is queer,'[6] Suppa said. 'The journeys the characters are on are inherently queer-coded; almost every NPC we will ever meet is queer; our characters and their families have fluid approaches to gender, family structure, sexuality – everything! Playing in a world that dazzles you in the blinding headlights of everything that is anti-heteronormative is really quite delightful. Most worlds are still cishet as default, so in *Trisha's Hideous Queers*, ours isn't.' Taylor Hunt also added that, as a DM, world-builder, and homebrewer, he's more focused on queer joy – and that means keeping bigotry out of his games. 'I am not interested in building worlds where queerness is an issue,'[7] he said. 'That doesn't mean that players or NPCs can't struggle to come to terms with their queerness if that's something people are interested in exploring, but no one is going to discriminate based on gender or sexuality.' With D&D,

queer folks can create and play in alternative worlds – and Taylor Hunt says that this is something that's compelling for him as well as other queer nerds. 'I'd say that queerness is inherently a state of no assumptions, of questioning norms, and finding your own path. That's why queers love D&D in general I reckon, and that's why I love homebrew collaborative world-building and campaign-writing – because you can create anything.'

In addition to *Trisha's Hideous Queers*, a couple of queer actual plays I find particularly exciting include: *Try Not to Die*, a self-described 'queer as hell'[8] D&D actual play; *Queens of Adventure*, which combines D&D with drag queens; and *Death2Divinity*, another actual play, in their own words, 'starring fat, queer babes'.[9] In a space where you can create anything, the possibilities to find your people, and then create incredible fantasy worlds, is endless.

Moving over to the social media realm of Twitter, a plethora of talented queer illustrators and painters are posting their work, taking commissions from folk who want their characters to be brought to life, and, in the process, creating a following who value seeing art that's at the intersection of the fantastical and the queer (of which there is often a large overlap).

An LGBTQIA+ artist whose work I especially admire is Jax (@gildedruin) – a Pacific Northwest-based lesbian who goes by they/she pronouns and whose art centres on sapphic intimacy. Their work is tender, emotive, and otherworldly. For instance, my favourite illustration of theirs is cut into 4 scenes: in the top left, two hands gently embrace upon what looks like bedsheets, or a cloak laid on the floor; in the top right, a half-elf kisses a human on the nose, their arms and breasts close to one another; in the bottom left, the human tugs the half-elf's cloak fastening, as if angry or lustful; in the bottom right, they kiss deeply, arms wrapped around one another.[10] Overall, this piece – like much of Jax's art – is in my opinion unabashedly queer, visually depicting common wants – intimacy, closeness, comfort.

On top of creating and posting her own work, they also retweet and share arresting works by others, creating a kind of illustrated hub of sapphic love, affinity, and joy; a place of optimism and hope, when homophobia and transphobia are on the rise in the real world. According to figures obtained by *VICE World News*, for example, homophobic hate crime reports in the UK have tripled in the last six years, while transphobic hate crime reports have quadrupled.[11]

For those looking to discover more LGBTQIA+ artists behind incredible queer and queer-coded characters, here are some more of my favourites: Kate Draws (@tacticiankate), who focuses on fantasy character design; Emi (@emisartcr), who draws D&D and TTRPG character art as well as environment concept art; and Tay (@Lynaiss), whose characters have a wonderfully powerful, regal air. There are innumerable creators out there, though, who are crafting art that makes D&D more vibrant, engaging, and welcoming.

As we can see, in the D&D space, LGBTQIA+ content creators and homebrewers are impacting both the present and the future for the better. By creating such work – and having them bought, enjoyed, shared, liked, commented on, discussed, and most important of all, seen by a wide range of people – queer representation and inclusion has been improved in and around a game that was notorious for being played by a certain type of person for decades. It's exciting, then, to think about what's in store in the future – what could we see and enjoy going forward?

Having queer-centred works publicly available has been – and will continue to be – an effective way of staking claim to the fact that Dungeons & Dragons isn't just for cishet guys, but for all kinds of people. To boot, it's through people flocking to these LGBTQIA+ materials, creators, topics, discussions, pages, and profiles – which the internet and social media, for all their pitfalls, have enabled – that the queer D&D community has grown and expanded into something louder, more prominent, more visible. It means that those seeking more from their adventures and their own interactions with D&D can find new worlds, and new people with whom to play with in those worlds. It means that those not quite ready or aren't sure where to start can have entry points that directly speak to them. All this inspires hope, as LGBTQIA+ nerds can more easily find each other, collaborate, connect, and revel in queerness in one of their preferred ways; with swords and sorcery in incredible settings laden with potentiality.

In many ways, there's historically been no better time to be a queer D&D fan than right now – and we've got to thank the queer community – which includes everyone, from queer homebrewers and content creators publishing their creations to fans who amplify the voices of other queer nerds – for their work; they're helping pave the way forward to an even queerer future for D&D. Of course, that's not to say that there was a sect of queer people who sat down at their desks and devised a tactical battle plan on how to make D&D more approachable and fun for queer people via homebrewed materials and posting beautiful illustrations on Twitter. Rather, it's been queer folks unapologetically being themselves, tapping into their imaginations and creativity, and sharing their magical queerness with the world via the internet that has made all this possible. It's a coalescing; a combination of queerness, creativity, and technological advancement in tandem. And we're here for it.

Another short rest

The end is near, adventurer; I can sense it – and perhaps you can, too. But before embarking on the final leg of our short quest, let's set up camp for one last rest. As we drink from our waterskins, I'd like to impart a few words on what to expect...

As we've discovered and learned from our journey thus far, Dungeons & Dragons is full of potential and can provide queer folk – marginalised humans who've historically been pushed to the edges of the society, often undervalued and underestimated by the majority – with the tools to explore and revel in queerness. Even video games, a much-loved pastime for many humans, cannot compare to the potentiality available and offered in Dungeons & Dragons. To boot, D&D can indisputably be a bastion of unbridled joy, fun, and creativity.

But, despite Dungeons & Dragons' many, many

positives and almost utopian potential that we've uncovered thus far, there are some aspects in D&D's official materials that can be defined as problematic.

Adventurer, we cannot talk about Dungeons & Dragons' incredible potential and myriad positives without talking about it in its entirety, warts and all, and so we'll next be investigating and analysing a selection of facets within the game, looking at the problems they can present or the issues they can contribute to.

After that, we'll reach the end of our journey – but not before reflecting on all that we've learned, and considering a brilliantly bright future for queerness and D&D.

Now that we've rested and regained our strength, it's time to put our packs and boots back on; our quest is nearly complete.

Part Three

Queer D&D's past, present, and future

Chapter 8
Problems & Hope

'You will find no pretentious dictums herein, no baseless limits arbitrarily placed on female strength or male charisma, no ponderous combat systems for greater "realism",' stated Gary Gygax in the preface for the 1978 Advanced Dungeons & Dragons *Players Handbook*.[1] Readers, however, would find themselves disappointed no more than three pages later: as it states in the 'Character Abilities (Strength)' section of the text, 'Ability Score: 14: Maximum strength possible for a female halfling character; Ability Score: 15: Maximum strength possible for a female gnome character [...]; Ability Score 16: Maximum strength possible for a female elf character,'[2] and so on, until other races like dwarves, humans, and half-orcs are covered – all of whom, according to the rules stipulated here, cannot be as strong as men of the same race.[3] Despite Gygax's proclamations that there weren't going to be any 'baseless' limitations, it's quickly proven that there undoubtedly were. In any consideration of the queer culture of D&D, it's important to look at and analyse how certain aspects of the official materials have been problematic for LGBTQIA+ D&D lovers, both then and now, for the full picture.

While, in later editions, there aren't such instances of gender-based Strength limitation, this textual moment within the game's official materials is one example of something that's inherently and needlessly exclusive. When it comes to official materials for Dungeons & Dragons, there have been multiple problematic moments in regard to gender, race, and queerness. But what are the things — such as dungeon rooms and language — that have or could push LGBTQIA+ folks away and leave them reeling, instead of bringing them in and facilitating a greater, more enjoyable gaming experience? Here, we'll dive into a few examples from Dungeons & Dragons' history to show what's come before.

In 1979, the *Dungeon Masters Guide* for 1e was released. Inside the compendium contained the minutiae around playing and conducting Dungeons & Dragons as a Dungeon Master; from how ageing works to how to facilitate aerial combat should it arise, to lists of useable potions to the types of monsters a party might encounter during their adventures. In the 'Treasure (Miscellaneous Magic)' section, page 145 specifically, there's the 'Girdle of Femininity/Masculinity' – the description of which is as follows: 'This broad leather band appears to be a normal belt used commonly by all sorts of adventurers, but of course it is magical. If buckled on, it will *immediately* change the sex of its wearer to the opposite gender. Its magical curse fulfilled, the belt then loses all power. The original sex of the character cannot be restored by any normal means, although a *wish* might do so (50% chance), and a powerful being can alter the situation, i.e., it takes a god-like creature to set matters aright with certainty. 10% of these girdles actually remove *all* sex from the wearer.'[4]

In these sentences alone, there are numerous issues which we could dissect and discuss – not least both 'sex' and 'gender' being used here to mean the same thing – but let's talk about the Girdle being a 'cursed' item. Over on the *Cannibal Halfling Gaming* blog, Maria Fanning wrote an article on the Girdle, talking about the Girdle's cursedness nearly straight away: '*The Girdle of Femininity/Masculinity* is a curse item. As what was seen by many trans players back in this time as the closest thing to acknowledgement of them in the "*World's Greatest Roleplaying Game*", the sheer fact alone that it is classified as a curse item should show you what the game back in those days thought of people like me. We

– trans people – are not a good thing. It says that we cannot be in this world naturally, and any existence of us is against our own choice and will and is instead something misfortune throws upon us.[5]

'This blends well into the harmful myths of trans people: that we are wolves in sheep's clothing, unsound of mind, or simply too naïve to know better. All harmful and untrue ideas of the trans experience.'[6]

My assumption is that the Girdle was intended and implemented to be a cheap gag, a way for a group of cishet guys to laugh at, say, Uth'gir the dwarf man played by John turning into Uth'gir the dwarf woman – whose appearance of course will be up to the Dungeon Master. But for those who are exploring queerness through their character, stumbling upon such an item can be troubling if not outright harmful; the player has no control over the change if they equip the belt – they don't have any input nor can they give their blessing. On this point, Fanning noted, 'It removes consent. The item is not something a trans adventurer in the world of Faerun would pick up to help themselves feel more at home in their body. It is a prank at its most generous interpretation and a punishment at its worst.'[7] There's also the fact that the description says '10% of these girdles actually remove *all* sex from the wearer'.[8] This implies that, what's even funnier or more outrageous is being in-between or outside of the concept of the male-female binary.

The Girdle of Femininity/Masculinity, then, is an item that thoughtful, considerate DMs would avoid from placing in their games. However, and with queer theorist Eve Kosofsky Sedgwick's idea of reparative reading in mind, is there the potential to reimagine a problematic item like the Girdle for the better – where, in your campaign, the newly imagined item isn't cursed, is easily investigable, entirely optional, and potentially helps queer adventurers rather than harms?

The Tomb of Horrors, an adventure written by Gary Gygax and published in 1978, has a longstanding reputation: it's regarded as one of the most difficult official adventures to complete and outlive due to the crypt's many lethal puzzles and hazardous traps. As David M. Ewalt wrote in his book *Of Dice and Men*, '[T]he adventure was meant to challenge out-of-control players, putting their outrageously powerful D&D characters to the test—and, hopefully, killing them. [...] Few survive long enough to collect any treasure, and even fewer manage to find their way back through the deadly maze and escape with their spoils.'[9] In 2017, Wizards of the Coast released *Tales from the Yawning Portal* – a collection of previously published, official adventures that had been altered to fit with modern-day 5e rules. Considering *Tomb of Horrors*' established reputation, its inclusion in the anthology would surely make for an entertaining experience for newbies and veterans alike, no?

While the adventure may indeed be enjoyable for some – if such a tricky, puzzle- and trap-based adventure suits your tastes, of course – there's a particular part of the tomb that can potentially put an end to the fun for some folks: a misty archway containing a portal to a room where adventurers' 'sex and alignment are reversed by a powerful magic'.[10] Exiting and then going back into the room undoes the change but also causes psychic damage, while entering the room a third time 'will reverse sex again. Only a *wish* spell will restore both alignment and sex.'[11]

The writer and Ph.D. student Christine Prevas, whose academic subject matter is trans horror, had been watching an actual play where a player's character set foot in this room. Over on *PanopLit*, and in an article titled 'D&D's Trouble with Trans Characters', Christine stated: 'I had to pause the video and confirm with a friend who had also watched. Yes, that's right: adapted for 5th edition in 2017 in the collection *Tales from the Yawning Portal*, "Tomb of Horrors" includes a room that, upon entry, "reverses" your character's physical sex and alignment — whatever "reverse" means, with regards to sex.[12]

'I couldn't help but think: what does "reverse sex" mean for a trans character? What would one of my characters do, in that situation? A trans character forced back into a body that makes them dysphoric? A nonbinary character for whom there isn't, exactly, a "reverse" or "opposite" sex?'[13]

This room in *Tomb of Horrors* can be defined as problematic for the very same reasons that the Girdle of Femininity/Masculinity can: it forcibly and non-consensually changes a character, who may be an avatar or extension of the player themselves. And, unless you've played or read about the module before, you may not know that such a space exists.

In Prevas' article, they went on to describe their thoughts and feelings after watching that moment in the actual play unfold: 'In a terrible wave of understanding, I realised this: *Tomb of Horrors* was updated for 5e mechanics, but it wasn't updated for 5e sensibilities. Or maybe that 5e wasn't as welcoming to trans characters as it pretended to be.'[14] Conscious DMs would avoid having such a room – or revaluate and reinterpret how it works. Instead, perhaps the room temporarily changes alignment – from, say, lawful good to chaotic evil – but nothing else. Or, if the misty archway is walked through, perhaps the room does nothing but the mist itself causes the adventurers to become sticky and anything they touch to stick to them – making for hilarity and difficulty in equal measure. If they're sneaking along a corridor with their backs to the wall, perhaps they get stuck there, necessitating some kind of check to see if they can free themselves from said wall single-handedly. What I'm getting at here is there are many other alternatives that could be implemented – and many that would be an improvement. If the cheap gag, or indeed shock value, was part of the goal, there's a lot of ways to achieve that without potentially causing harm.

Earlier, I mentioned Corellon Larethian – the chief deity of elves, who was first brought into D&D cannon in 1980's *Deities & Demigods*, accompanying Advanced Dungeons & Dragons.

When the *Player's Handbook* for 5e was introduced, Corellon was once again mentioned, this time in the 'personality and background' section of the book. The text concerning Corellon was as follows: 'You don't need to be confined to binary notions of sex and gender. The elf god Corellon Larethian is often seen as androgynous or hermaphroditic, for example, and some elves in the multiverse are made in Corellon's image.'[15] While there must've been the intent to say to players something along the lines of *queer characters, including non-binary and also intersex folks, exist in the worlds of Dungeons & Dragons, so feel free for your characters to be queer, too*, the writing missed several marks. Not least because the term 'hermaphroditic' is a dehumanising and medicalising term, and androgyny isn't a gender identity but rather an aesthetic and presentation – after all, you don't have to look like David Bowie or Grace Jones to be non-binary.

Feedback on the use of 'hermaphroditic' got back to Wizards, however, as the term was taken out. Still, the word 'androgynous' continues to feature. While Jeremy Crawford stated on Twitter that Corellon isn't non-binary representation,[16] it still feels as if, simply with the word appearing where it does, that the writers are conflating androgyny with being non-binary.

Ultimately, while it's clear that Wizards acknowledge that diversity, inclusion, and representation in their game materials are important and necessary, the Corellon debacle in the 5e *Player's Handbook* seems like an attempt that has fallen and still falls short. Going forward, the solution would be to simply provide references to queer characters in official D&D materials like the aforementioned Fala Lefaliir from *Waterdeep: Dragon Heist*, alongside accurate and appropriate wording to denote who and what those characters are, with a louder statement encouraging the player to create queer characters if they want to. And, with the next edition of Dungeons & Dragons and the next *Player's Handbook*, perhaps we'll see that happen.

'One of the explicit design goals of 5th edition D&D is to depict humanity in all its beautiful diversity by depicting characters who represent an array of ethnicities, gender identities, sexual orientations, and beliefs',[17] the company said in their article 'Diversity and Dungeons & Dragons'. 'We want everyone to feel at home around the game table and to see positive reflections of themselves within our products.'[18]

'We'd like to share with you what we've been doing, and what we plan to do in the future to address legacy D&D content that does not reflect who we are today'[19], they also said in the piece. 'We recognize that doing this isn't about getting to a place where we can rest on our laurels but continuing to head in the right direction. We feel that being transparent about it is the best way to let our community help us to continue to calibrate our efforts.'[20]

The post went on to point out the changes, amendments, and actions the company were and are taking – from incorporating sensitivity readers into their creative process when creating official material for D&D, to presenting certain game races such as drow and orcs in a more nuanced light in official material, and changing racially insensitive text in the *Curse of Strahd* and *Tomb of Annihilation* adventures. Races in fantasy, unfortunately, can be depicted with harmful stereotypes, generalisations, and caricatures – this was the case with the Vistani, a people in *Curse of Strahd* whose depiction evoked reductive tropes of Earth's Romani people.

The fact that work is being done by Wizards on such fronts and to right past wrongs is promising, but it's also an ongoing journey that can't happen overnight. On the subject of journeys, throughout this book, I've consciously tried to focus on the myriad possibilities for play, exploration, and joy that Dungeons & Dragons offers queer people – the many positives from an enormously fun game that's simply like no other. But, acknowledging some of the more problematic parts of its history – and also showing how it's evolving – was necessary, just as progressive change is necessary. To fully understand the potential of where we are and where we could go, we needed to consider what has come before, even if some of those facets are now relegated to the game's history.

At its core, D&D allows folks to create and be part of much better, brighter, and freer worlds than those on Earth – an amazing, powerful thing which all materials should reflect. In my mind, Dungeons & Dragons has an almost utopian potential for queer folks – a game that's revolutionary in its scope, and can be revolutionary for its players. Most notably, at the right tables and as long as they're comfortable to do so, queer people can conduct their own investigations into gender and/or sexuality with their characters – or just revel in it! – all while 'getting to be an absolute badass'[21] as Fiona Reid said earlier. Perhaps somebody begins playing a character who's a badass non-binary elf rogue – and perhaps playing that character helps them realise that they're badass and non-binary in real life, too. Dungeons & Dragons already intersects with queerness in many beautiful and fruitful ways. And if this is the trajectory of Wizards' game going forward – seeking to improve and being truly, fully inclusive – then that's the most exciting future imaginable.

Conclusion
As one journey ends, another begins

Adventurer, all the paths we've travelled down have led us to this – the end of our short quest. While there's no chest of gold coins to be opened, nor are there any magical items for you to keep (apart from this book!), that doesn't mean you're leaving empty-handed. We've both been bestowed with perhaps the greatest reward of all: knowledge.

We've learned that, in the early '70s, Dungeons & Dragons was released unto the world – and it quickly took it by storm. You can create and play incredible characters who can manipulate magic or know how to efficiently use weapons like swords and shields; you can explore imaginative worlds and magnificent environs; you can defeat treacherous foes in tense combat; you can have a profound impact on the people in these worlds and drive the plot; you can ultimately save the day with your friends – all massively intoxicating, engaging things for nerds. We've also looked at how, mechanically, the game has been periodically updated, with 5e making the game potentially the most accessible and streamlined it's ever been. And we've explored what's drawn people to the game in contemporary times, in turn helping its popularity to reach heady new heights.

But the bulk of our learnings, adventurer, have been related to D&D and queerness specifically. We've since learned how LGBTQIA+ folks and queerness became more prominent in and around the game (which is a reason to rejoice in itself), what's contributed to the game's more queer-friendly image shift, on top of looking at some problematic elements in D&D's history. Perhaps most importantly, though, we've analysed and celebrated the gameplay elements that can be especially beneficial and/or enjoyable for LGBTQIA+ D&D players – and we've done so in more than a purely academic sense. People in this book have explained how the game has played a part in their own journeys – and there are countless similar (and also different!) stories out there.

Before writing this book, it was my firm belief that Dungeons & Dragons can be especially powerful for queer folks – and it was something I believed on an instinctive level from very early on. In truth, researching and writing *They Came to Slay* has only strengthened my conviction. Now, there's no doubt in my mind that Dungeons & Dragons can be a phenomenal game for LGBTQIA+ people. Not least because, as we've uncovered together:

1. People can play with, experiment with, and lean into queerness thanks to player characters and NPCs.
2. Having player characters and NPCs in D&D can give people a safeguarded, less pressured way to play with, experiment with, and lean into queerness.
3. Worlds in D&D can be free from the things that make life harder for LGBTQIA+ people back on Earth – such as biphobia, homophobia, transphobia, racism, ableism, and other forms of oppression.
4. In these worlds, a D&D group can interact with and revel in queerness on a scale that they might not be able to in real life.
5. Going on wild, outlandish adventures with your friends for a few hours each week is out-and-out fun and provides respite from day-to-day life on contemporary planet Earth.

Suffice to say, as a game, Dungeons & Dragons is absolutely brimming with queer potentiality – and hopefully, after making the jump to somebody who's written (or rather DM'd!) a short book on D&D and queerness, I've also helped you to get excited about D&D in a queer context, too. And this book has been just a small snapshot of queerness in and around D&D – there's so much more out there.

While on the topic of exciting things, what's particularly thrilling is the fact that the future of D&D is unwritten. If you were to ask me what I envisage for D&D's future, I'd have to say I see even more queerness – and a *lot* of slaying.

I've done enough talking, adventurer – it's time to bid each other farewell and begin new, separate journeys. If you're new to D&D or you haven't yet played, I hope you'll soon find a group you click with, and with whom you can experience the highs of D&D yourself. If you're already a D&D lover, I wish all your rolls to be natural 20s – apart from the times when it's objectively hilarious to roll a nat 1. And if you're a queer D&D player or soon-to-be player, I hope your future games are boundlessly joyful. Because boundless joy can absolutely be gleaned from the spellbinding, enchanting game that is Dungeons & Dragons.

References

Chapter 1

1. "Dungeon Master: The Life and Legacy of Gary Gygax." David Kushner, *WIRED*, 10 March 2008. web.archive.org/web/20090129141050/http://www.wired.com/gaming/virtualworlds/news/2008/03/ff_gygax?currentPage=3. Accessed 7 January 2022.
2. "Gary Gygax, co-creator of Dungeons & Dragons game." Emily Fredrix, *The Boston Globe*, 5 March 2008. archive.boston.com/bostonglobe/obituaries/articles/2008/03/05/gary_gygax_co_creator_of_dungeons__dragons_game/. Accessed 28 April 2022.
3. "History: Forty Years of Adventure." Jon Peterson, *Dungeons & Dragons*. dnd.wizards.com/dungeons-and-dragons/what-dd/history/history-forty-years-adventure. Accessed 7 January 2022.
4. David M. Ewalt, *Of Dice and Men*. Scribner, 2013. p63.
5. Ibid. p61.
6. "Dungeon Master: The Life and Legacy of Gary Gygax." David Kushner, *WIRED*, 10 March 2008. web.archive.org/web/20090129141050/http://www.wired.com/gaming/virtualworlds/news/2008/03/ff_gygax?currentPage=3. Accessed 7 January 2022.

7. "The Story of D&D Part One: The Birth, Death, and Resurrection of Dungeons & Dragons." Ben Riggs, *Nerdist*, 26 December 2017. nerdist.com/article/the-story-of-dd-part-one-the-birth-death-and-resurrection-of-dungeons-dragons/. Accessed 7 January 2022.
8. David M. Ewalt, *Of Dice and Men*. Scribner, 2013. p65.
9. "Dungeon Master: The Life and Legacy of Gary Gygax." David Kushner, *WIRED*, 10 March 2008. web.archive.org/web/20090129141050/http://www.wired.com/gaming/virtualworlds/news/2008/03/ff_gygax?currentPage=3. Accessed 7 January 2022.
10. David M. Ewalt, *Of Dice and Men*. Scribner, 2013. p70-71.
11. "History: Forty Years of Adventure." Jon Peterson, *Dungeons & Dragons*. dnd.wizards.com/dungeons-and-dragons/what-dd/history/history-forty-years-adventure. Accessed 7 January 2022.
12. "Dungeon Master: The Life and Legacy of Gary Gygax." David Kushner, *WIRED*, 10 March 2008. web.archive.org/web/20090129141050/http://www.wired.com/gaming/virtualworlds/news/2008/03/ff_gygax?currentPage=3. Accessed 7 January 2022.
13. "History: Forty Years of Adventure." Jon Peterson, *Dungeons & Dragons*. dnd.wizards.com/dungeons-and-dragons/what-dd/history/history-forty-years-adventure. Accessed 7 January 2022.
14. "Tsr Hobbies Mixes Fact And Fantasy." Stewart Alsop II, *Inc.*, 1 February 1982. inc.com/magazine/19820201/3601.html. Accessed 8 January 2022.
15. David M. Ewalt, *Of Dice and Men*. Scribner, 2013. p174.
16. "History: Forty Years of Adventure." Jon Peterson, *Dungeons & Dragons*. dnd.wizards.com/dungeons-and-dragons/what-dd/history/history-forty-years-adventure. Accessed 7 January 2022.
17. "Dungeons and Dragons Infographic Shows How Popular the Game Has Become." Cameron Corliss, *Game Rant*, 19

May 2021. gamerant.com/dungeons-and-dragons-infographic-2021/. Accessed 8 January 2022.
18. Bonnie Ruberg, *Video Games Have Always Been Queer*. New York University Press, 2019. p7.

Chapter 2

1. Gary Gygax, *Players Handbook*. Wizards of the Coast, 2012. p9.
2. Ibid.
3. Gwendolyn Marshall, Zoom interview. 19 April 2022.
4. "The Draw of Destiny | Critical Role | Campaign 3, Episode 1." Critical Role, *YouTube*, 25 October 2021. youtube.com/watch?v=P8pLvV3FjPc. Accessed 10 November 2021.

Chapter 3

1. "Dungeons & Dragons Promises To Make Its Adventures More Queer." Cecilia D'Anastasio, *Kotaku*, 24 August 2017. kotaku.com/dungeons-dragons-promises-to-make-the-game-more-queer-1798401117. Accessed 7 January 2022.
2. Ibid.
3. *Waterdeep: Dragon Heist*. Michele Carter, Scott Fitzgerald Gray, Kim Mohan, Wizards of the Coast, 2018. p32.
4. *Player's Handbook*. Jeremy Crawford, James Wyatt, Robert J. Schwalb, Bruce R. Cordell, Wizards of the Coast, 2018. p121.
5. "The Story of D&D Part Two: How Wizards of the Coast Saved Dungeons & Dragons." Ben Riggs, *Nerdist*, 27 December 2017. nerdist.com/article/the-story-of-dd-part-two-how-wizards-of-the-coast-saved-dungeons-dragons/. Accessed 7 January 2022.
6. "Celebrating Pride and LGBTQ+ Players and Employees at Wizards." Jontelle Leyson-Smith, *Dungeons & Dragons*,

      1 June 2021. company.wizards.com/en/news/celebrating-pride-and-lgbtq-players-2021. Accessed 18 February 2022.
7. Ibid.
8. Anthony Rapp, Zoom interview. 4 May 2022.
9. "Wizards Celebrates and Supports Pride." *Dungeons & Dragons*, 1 June 2021. company.wizards.com/en/news/wizards-celebrates-pride-2021. Accessed 18 February 2022.
10. Ibid.
11. "Celebrating Pride and LGBTQ+ Players and Employees at Wizards." Jontelle Leyson-Smith, *Dungeons & Dragons*, 1 June 2021. company.wizards.com/en/news/celebrating-pride-and-lgbtq-players-2021. Accessed 18 February 2022.
12. Ibid.
13. "Finding Your Place in D&D | Pride Roundtable 2021 w/ Star Trek's Anthony Rapp | D&D Beyond." D&D Beyond, *YouTube*, 21 June 2021. youtube.com/watch?v=_ajcoyS792w. Accessed 28 February 2022.
14. Ibid.

Chapter 4

1. "Sharkfolk (5e Race)." *D&D Wiki*, publish date unknown. dandwiki.com/wiki/Sharkfolk_(5e_Race). Accessed 4 January 2022.
2. "Mousefolk (5e Race)." *D&D Wiki*, publish date unknown. dandwiki.com/wiki/Mousefolk_(5e_Race). Accessed 4 January 2022.
3. Gwendolyn Marshall, Zoom interview. 19 April 2022.
4. Lynne M. Meyer, email interview. 2 May 2022.
5. Fiona Reid, email interview. 10 May 2022.

Chapter 5

1. Daniel Mackay, *The Fantasy Role-Playing Game: A New Performing Art*. McFarland & Company, Inc., Publishers, 2001. p2.
2. Richard Schechner, *Between Theater & Anthropology*. University of Pennsylvania Press, 1985. p49 (via Google Books).
3. Ibid.
4. Anthony Rapp, Zoom interview. 4 May 2022.
5. Posey Mehta, digital interview. 22 April 2022.

Chapter 6

1. Gavin McMurtrie, email interview. 29 March 2022.
2. Robbie Taylor Hunt, digital interview. 21 April 2022.
3. Gavin McMurtrie, email interview. 29 March 2022.
4. Anthony Rapp, Zoom interview. 4 May 2022.
5. Gavin McMurtrie, email interview. 29 March 2022.

Chapter 7

1. Oliver Darkshire, *Queercoded*. Self-published on Dungeon Masters Guild, 2021. p1.
2. "Queercoded." Oliver Darkshire, *Dungeon Masters Guild*, 9 March 2021. dmsguild.com/product/349605/Queercoded. Accessed 24 February 2022.
3. Ibid.
4. *Player's Handbook*. Jeremy Crawford, James Wyatt, Robert J. Schwalb, Bruce R. Cordell, Wizards of the Coast, 2018. p280.
5. Robbie Taylor Hunt, digital interview. 21 April 2022.
6. Rosanna Suppa, digital interview. 21 April 2022.
7. Robbie Taylor Hunt, digital interview. 21 April 2022.
8. twitter.com/trynottodiepod

9. twitter.com/Death2Divinity_
10. gildedruin.carrd.co
11. "'Don't Punish Me For Who I Am': Huge Jump In Anti-LGBTQ Hate Crime Reports in UK." Ben Hunte, *VICE*, 11 October 2021. vice.com/en/article/4avkyw/anti-lgbtq-hate-crime-reports-increase-in-six-years. Accessed 25 February 2022.

Chapter 8

1. Gary Gygax, *Players Handbook*. Wizards of the Coast, 2012. p6.
2. Ibid, p9.
3. Ibid.
4. Gary Gygax, *Dungeon Masters Guide*. Wizards of the Coast, 2012. p145.
5. "Rolling for Gender: Why I'm Angry At A D&D 1st Edition Magic Item." Maria Fanning, *Cannibal Halfling Gaming*, 9 October 2020. cannibalhalflinggaming.com/2020/10/09/why-im-angry-at-a-dd-1st-edition-magic-item/. Accessed 7 October 2021.
6. Ibid.
7. Ibid.
8. Gary Gygax, *Dungeon Masters Guide*. Wizards of the Coast, 2012. p145.
9. David M. Ewalt, *Of Dice and Men*. Scribner, 2013. p144.
10. *Tales from the Yawning Portal*. Kim Mohan, Mike Mearls, Wizards of the Coast, 2017. p219.
11. Ibid.
12. "D&D's Trouble with Trans Characters." Christine Prevas, *PanopLit*, 13 February 2018. panoplit.org/2018/02/13/dds-trouble-with-trans-characters/. Accessed 7 October 2021.
13. Ibid.
14. Ibid.

15. *Queerness in Play*. Todd Harper, Meghan Blythe Adams, Nicholas Taylor, Palgrave Macmillan, 2018. p166 (via Google Books).
16. "Corellon is not a representation of nonbinary people or an attempt to represent being genderfluid. Corellon is a magical god who is physically fluid in every way, including sex. Being queer (as many of us are) requires no magic and no elven gods. We are gloriously real." @jeremyecrawford. *Twitter*, 28 December 2018, 11:14pm, twitter.com/jeremyecrawford/status/1078791346763321345. Accessed 7 October 2021.
17. "Diversity and Dungeons & Dragons." *Dungeons & Dragons*, 17 June 2020. dnd.wizards.com/news/diversity-and-dnd. Accessed 7 October 2021.
18. Ibid.
19. Ibid.
20. Ibid.
21. Fiona Reid, email interview. 10 May 2022.

Acknowledgements

A huge thanks, first and foremost, to Heather McDaid and Laura Jones at 404 Ink. Thank you, both, for deciding to commission and go ahead with this Inkling. It's been an incredible opportunity, and for that, I'll always be grateful. I'm also very grateful for the editorial expertise and advice along the way, and the help with turning my drafts into a proper, actual book!

Similarly, I'd like to thank everybody I interviewed and spoke to for this book – for your time, for your insight, for your help, and for your support. There were so many thought-provoking and inspiring conversations, and I'd happily have those conversations (and conversations like them!) all day, every day.

I'd like to thank everybody I've played Dungeons & Dragons with so far (and shoutout to the folks I'll inevitably play with in the future!) – there's no way I'd rather spend my time than playing and nerding out over

Dungeons & Dragons, which very much feels like a privilege.

I'd also like to thank my family and friends for helping foster an interest in fantasy and nerdery since an early age; fantasy has been a constant thread in my life, and one that'll surely keep going and keep bringing me joy.

Lastly, I'd like to thank you, the reader, for reading and buying a copy of *They Came to Slay*. It means the world.

About the Author

Thom James Carter is a writer based in Scotland. His work has been published by the *New Statesman*, *Current Affairs*, *WIRED*, *Insider*, *Wellcome Collection*, and more. He holds a B.A. in English and an M.A. in Creative Writing, both from Goldsmiths, University of London.

About the Inklings series

This book is part of 404 Ink's Inkling series which presents big ideas in pocket-sized books.

They are all available at 404ink.com/shop.

If you enjoyed this book, you may also enjoy these titles in the series:

Love That Journey For Me: The Queer Revolution of *Schitt's Creek* – Emily Garside

Love That Journey For Me dives deep into the cultural sensation of Canadian comedy-drama *Schitt's Creek*. Considering the fusion of existing sitcom traditions, references and tropes, this Inkling analyses the nuance of the show and its surrounding cultural and societal impact as a queer revolution.

The End: Surviving the World Through Imagined Disasters – Katie Goh

The End studies apocalypse fiction and its role in how we manage, manifest and imagine social, economic and political disaster and crises. What do apocalypse narratives tell us about how we imagine our place in history? Why do we fantasise about the end of the world? What does this all unveil about our contemporary anxieties?

The Loki Variations: The Man, The Myth, The Mischief – Karl Johnson

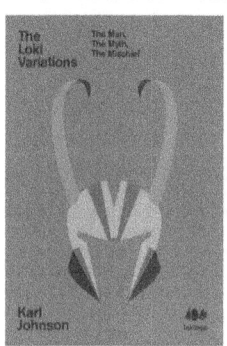

Loki, ever the shapeshifter, has never been more adaptable across pop culture. By exploring contemporary variations of Loki, from Norse god to antihero trickster, we can better understand the power of myth, queer theory, fandom, ritual, pop culture itself and more.